The M*A*S*H Trivia Quiz Book

The M*A*S*H Trivia Quiz Book

by Cristopher & Ryan DeRose

BearManor Media
2019

The M*A*S*H Trivia Quiz Book

© 2019 Cristopher DeRose and Ryan DeRose

All rights reserved.

No portion of this publication may be reproduced, stored, and/or copied electronically (except for academic use as a source), nor transmitted in any form or by any means without the prior written permission of the publisher and/or author.

Published in the United States of America by:

BearManor Media

4700 Millenia Blvd.
Suite 175 PMB 90497
Orlando, FL 32839

bearmanormedia.com

Printed in the United States.

Typesetting and layout by John Teehan

ISBN—978-1-62933-490-5

For Lois. Again

Table of Contents

Attention, All Personnel!..................................1

Season One...5
Season Two 37
Season Three..63
Season Four...89
Season Five...113
Season Six..137
Season Seven..159
Season Eight..183
Season Nine 207
Season Ten..227
Season Eleven 249

Answers 267

Attention, All Personnel!

WHEN RICHARD HOOKER'S NOVEL *MASH: A Novel About Three Army Doctors* became first a movie, then a TV series, there were significant differences from Hooker's original vision to each retelling in the given media, but all made their presences known and felt decades later. (Richard Hooker was a *nom de plume* for Dr. H. Richard Hornberger, inspired by his experience as a surgeon during the Korean War, and his co-author W.C. Heinz, a sports writer and war correspondent.) Hooker would write the first sequel, *MASH Goes to Maine,* in 1972 and series of *MASH* books were written following the success of the TV series credited to Richard Hooker and William E. Butterworth, although Butterworth had written them alone. Hooker would be credited alone for only one other book in the series, *MASH Mania* in 1977.

MASH, which ran from September 17, 1972, to February 28, 1983, was seen in households that were very different from ours in 2019. *MASH* audiences of the 1970s were treated to some of the best television entertainment. It could be unflinching in its honest portrayal of war *and* make us laugh. It used some revolutionary means of storytelling. But most importantly, episodes such as "POV" (Season 7, Episode 11), "A War for All Seasons" (9.6), "Life Time" (8.11) or the rarely rerun "Dreams" (8.22) were not merely for creating spectacle on the small screen amidst flagging numbers of viewers. The stories always came first, and it showed in the viewership and critical respect the show garner over its eleven-season run. MASH was able to transcend generations in the storytelling subject and dynamics, resulting in the show never having been removed from heavy syndication in the years since its debut.

Which is what brings us to this book.

The trivia questions posed to the reader cover the show's entire run, including the series finale, "Farewell, Goodbye, and Amen." There can be as few as two questions per episode to a good deal more, depending on how detailed the authors considered a given episode. Of special note is that the source used has been the *MASH: Complete Collection* DVDs. Many episodes in syndication today have been edited to allow for more commercial time, and thus some things referred to in the questions will not be seen in syndication. Credits are as per IMDb.

Episodes are broken down by season, in broadcast order. At the top of each season, the regular cast members will be noted, with additional cast mentioned in specific episodes. Special attention has been given to note an early appearance of actors such as Ron Howard, George Wendt, John Ritter and Laurence Fishburne, to name but a few. Also noted are actors who made more than one appearance, more often than not as a different character.

For the sake of simplicity (and the sanity of the authors), characters are referred by the name most commonly used in the series, i.e.; Hawkeye, Henry, etc. In the case of Maj.

Houlihan, she is referred to as Hot Lips until the character's development sees her referred to more commonly as Margaret.

While the questions can range from easy to difficult, the authors want first and foremost the intent to be one of fun and appreciation. This is not meant as a comprehensive study of timelines and continuity or to point out historical/technical/regulation inaccuracies. The show was produced in a much different creative environment than the more interactive kind we see in contemporary fandom, and no TV show is perfect.

This was a joy to write, and while the show we're visiting had its stark moments, the enjoyment and appreciation of the series is the intent we hope you, the reader, share.

SEASON ONE

STARRING

Alan Alda as Capt. Benjamin Franklin "Hawkeye" Pierce

Wayne Rogers as Capt. "Trapper" John McIntyre

McLean Stevenson as Lt. Col. Henry Blake

Loretta Swit as Maj. Margaret "Hot Lips" Houlihan

Larry Linville as Maj. Frank Burns

Gary Burghoff as Cpl. Walter "Radar" O'Reilly

Trivia answers for Season One begin on page 267.

EPISODE 1.1 "Pilot"

Director: Gene Reynolds
Written by: Larry Gelbart

SELECTED SUPPORTING CAST
G. Wood as Brig. Gen Charlie Hammond
Patrick Adiarte as Ho-Jon
Karen Philipp as Lt. Maria "Dish" Schneider
George Morgan as Lt. Father Francis John Mulcahy
Timothy Brown as Capt. Oliver Harmon "Spearchucker" Jones
Odessa Cleveland as Lt. Ginger Bayliss
John Orchard as Capt. "Ugly" John Black

SYNOPSIS
Hawkeye holds a camp raffle to help houseboy Ho-Jon attend his alma mater. The prize? A weekend in Tokyo with nurse Lt. Maria "Dish" Schneider.

1. How long ago do the opening titles, (following "Korea, 1950") say how long ago it was?

2. What game is Radar playing when he announces the arrival of choppers?

3. During the opening credits, which arm of a wounded soldier hangs off the chopper pod?

4. During the opening credits, how many jeeps transport the wounded from the helipad?

5. What is Mulcahy's nickname (used only in this episode)?

6. How many hours does Hawkeye say they've been in surgery?

7. How much does Hawkeye sell the raffle tickets for?

8. What color is the military scrip Hawkeye and Trapper count?

9. What does Frank stumble over after getting thrown out of the Swamp?

10. What kind and color of hat does Mulcahy wear?

11. Who does Hot Lips call to come to the 4077th?

12. How much money does Hawkeye say the camp has raised for Ho-Jon?

13. What does Hawkeye say when he sees the heavily bandaged Frank come shambling, led by Hot Lips?

14. Ho-Jon's party is interrupted by the arrival of wounded. From which country are the soldiers noted as being from?

15. Which hand of Hawkeye's is handcuffed to Trapper?

EPISODE 1.2 "To Market, To Market"

Director: Michael O'Herlihy
Writer: Burt Styler

SELECTED SUPPORTING CAST
Jack Soo as Charlie Lee
Robert Ito as Lin
G. Wood as Gen. Hammond
Odessa Cleveland as Ginger
John C. Johnson as Truck Driver

You may recognize Jack Soo from being a cast member of another '70s TV hit, *Barney Miller*. He would appear in another *MASH* episode, "Payday" (3.22).

SYNOPSIS
When the black market hijacks the 4077's shipment of hydrocortisone, Hawkeye and Trapper seek other means of obtaining it.

1. Which kind of wood is Henry's desk?

2. Who does Hawkeye impersonate when calling Gen. Hammond?

3. Who does Hammond tell Henry he's meeting?

4. Which country's flag flies on the jeep Hawkeye and Trapper use?

5. How much does hydrocortisone get on the black market?

6. Which rank does Charlie impersonate when he meets with Henry?

7. How did Henry get the oversized desk into his office?

8. What does Frank thank Hot Lips for?

9. How do Hawkeye and Trapper get Henry's desk out of the office?

10. What is the name of the pilot who flies the desk to Charlie?

11. Henry, Hawkeye, and Trapper watch the desk fly away. What does Trapper ask Henry?

EPISODE 1.3 "Requiem for a Lightweight"

Director: Hy Averback
Writer: Robert Klane

SELECTED SUPPORTING CAST
Sorrell Booke as Gen. Barker
John Orchard as "Ugly" John
Marcia Strassman as Margie Cutler
William Christopher as Father Mulcahy

You may recognize Sorrell Booke from another TV series, *The Dukes of Hazzard.*

Marcia Strassman would go on to co-star in TV's *Welcome Back, Kotter,* and the feature film *Honey, I Shrunk the Kids.*

SYNOPSIS

When a new nurse proves to be a distraction, Hot Lips has her transferred. It's up to Hawkeye and Trapper to get her back by Trapper participating in a boxing match.

1. What does Trapper take of Frank's to give to Margie?

2. What is Margie doing when both Hawkeye and Trapper show up at her tent?

3. By what names does Henry call Hawkeye and Trapper?

4. Where does Trapper say he learned to fight?

5. Who is Trapper's less-than-enthusiastic sparring partner?

6. What does Hawkeye tell Trapper he has after Radar beats him?

7. Whose duffel bag is Trapper using as a heavy bag while training?

8. What drug does Ugly John apply to one of Trapper's gloves?

9. Which rank does Trapper's opponent hold?

10. What boxing nickname is on the back of Trapper's robe?

11. Who serves as timekeeper for the fight?

EPISODE 1.4 "Chief Surgeon Who?"

Director: E.W. Swackhamer
Writer: Larry Gelbart

SELECTED SUPPORTING CAST
Sorrell Booke as Gen. Barker
Timothy Brown as "Spearchucker" Jones
John Orchard as "Ugly" John
Jamie Farr as Klinger
Jack Riley as Capt. Kaplan
Linda Meiklejohn as Leslie
Bob Gooden as Boone
Odessa Cleveland as Ginger

SYNOPSIS
When Henry decides to name Hawkeye as chief surgeon, Hot Lips and Frank call Gen. Barker to review the surgeon's work.

1. What two things does Hawkeye hold at the start of the story?

2. How does Frank say he keeps in touch with patience from his stateside practice?

3. How many cars does Frank say he owns?

4. According to Frank, how many times has Hawkeye saluted him?

5. According to Henry, who is the best doctor in the camp?

6. During Hawkeye's "coronation" as chief surgeon, what item serves as his scepter?

7. How many leis does Radar wear during the coronation?

8. By what name does Hawkeye refer to Ugly John during their poker game?

9. What is Radar doing when Gen. Barker comes into Henry's office?

10. Who is on sentry duty during the coronation?

11. What foreign matter does Trapper find in the scrub sink?

EPISODE 1.5 "The Moose"

Director: Hy Averback
Writer: Laurence Marks

SELECTED SUPPORTING CAST
Paul Jenkins as Baker
Virginia Lee as Young-Hi
Timothy Brown as "Spearchucker" Jones

Virginia Lee would be seen in the episodes "Henry, Please Come Home" (1.9, uncredited), "Exorcism" (5.13) and "Welcome to Korea" (4.1).

SYNOPSIS
An American soldier visits the camp with his "moose," a Korean girl he has bought from her family to act as servant.

1. What is Baker's rank?

2. What word does Hawkeye tell Baker he doesn't care for?

3. With which poker hand does Hawkeye win Young-Hi from Baker?

4. What is Hawkeye doing when Baker brings Young-Hi to the Swamp?

5. How happy does Young-Hi tell Hawkeye he will be with her as his moose?

6. Who interrupts Hawkeye's date to tell him Young-Hi has returned?

7. How does Trapper describe Young-Hi?

8. What does Young-Hi say when Hawkeye tells her she's

beautiful?

9. What is Young-Hi's brother's name?

EPISODE 1.6 "Yankee Doodle Doctor"

Director: Lee Phillips
Writer: Laurence Marks

SELECTED SUPPORTING CAST
Ed Flanders as Lt. Bricker
Bert Kramer as Sgt. Martin
Marcia Strassman as Margie Cutler
Herb Voland as Col. Clayton

SYNOPSIS
Trapper and Hawkeye decide to make their own documentary about the realities of war when they realize the filmmaker assigned to them is more interested in propaganda.

1. What are Hawkeye and Trapper doing while Frank is shaving?

2. What is the rank and name of the filmmaker?

3. Which actor does Hawkeye impersonate when Bricker asks if he's ever done any acting?

4. What classic character does Frank say he played in college?

5. Who does Bricker ask to narrate his film?

6. From where in the Swamp does Trapper retrieve the script from?

7. Which comic acting legends do Hawkeye and Trapper impersonate in their film?

8. In their own film, what does Trapper hand to Hawkeye for the latter to use as a scalpel?

EPISODE 1.7 "Bananas, Crackers, and Nuts"

Director: Bruce Bilson
Writer: Burt Styler

SELECTED SUPPORTING CAST
Odessa Cleveland as Lt. Ginger Bayliss
Stuart Margolin as Capt. Sherman
Marcia Strassman Lt. Margie Cutler

SYNOPSIS
Hawkeye feigns a mental breakdown in order for him and Trapper to get some R&R. A psychiatrist who knows Hot Lips comes to evaluate him.

1. Where is Trapper sleeping when Hot Lips wakes him?

2. What does Trapper want after the long stretch in surgery?

3. How big of an olive does Hawkeye say would be in his and Trapper's martinis?

4. How many days does Trapper tell Hawkeye he should already have stored in his body?

5. Where is the R&R Center located?

6. What is Hawkeye wearing when he enters the mess tent with his meal?

7. What does Hawkeye tell Frank he's eating?

8. Who touches Hawkeye's plate?

9. What color pills does Trapper tell Radar to give to Hawkeye?

10. Who switches the sign on Hot Lip's tent?

EPISODE 1.8 "Cowboy"

Director: Don Weis
Writer: Bob Klane

SELECTED SUPPORTING CAST
William Christopher as Father Mulcahy
Billy Green Bush as John "Cowboy" Hodges
Patrick Adiarte as Ho-Jon

SYNOPSIS
Henry grows increasingly paranoid when it appears someone in the camp wants him dead.

1. Where is Cowboy wounded?

2. From where on Radar's body does Hawkeye tell him he'll remove his tonsils for waking him up?

3. What is the par on the first hole of the 4077's golf course?

4. Who acts as caddy for Hawkeye and Henry?

5. What comes crashing through Henry's tent?

6. What does Henry say after the latrine explodes while he's in it?

7. When tasting Henry's food for him, how much of it does Trapper eat?

8. Which article of Henry's office furniture explodes?

9. What is Cowboy's callsign?

10. What city is Cowboy from?

11. What causes Henry to spill his drink on himself?

EPISODE 1.9 "Henry Please Come Home"

Director: William Wiard
Writer: Laurence Marks

SELECTED SUPPORTING CAST
Odessa Cleveland as Lt. Ginger Bayliss
Patrick Adiarte as Ho-Jon
Timothy Brown as Capt. Oliver "Spearchucker" Jones
William Christopher as Father Francis Mulcahy
G. Wood as Brig. Gen. Hammond
Robert Gooden as Pvt. Boone

SYNOPSIS
Brig. Gen. Hammond transfers Henry to Tokyo, much to Frank's delight, and Hawkeye and Trapper's displeasure.

1. What song is sung in the OR during the opening scene?

2. Which nurse does Frank want brought up on the charge of insubordination?

3. What does the 4077's staff do when Henry says he doesn't have a speech?

4. Who wakes up the Swamp mates when the sounding of "Reveille" doesn't wake them up?

5. What does Frank say he wants out of the Swamp?

6. What does Pvt. Boone suggest they do to Frank to be rid of his command?

7. Who feigns illness to get Henry back to the 4077?

EPISODE 1.10 "I Hate a Mystery"

Director: Hy Averback
Writer: Hal Dresner

SELECTED SUPPORTING CAST
Patrick Adiarte as Ho-Jon
Timothy Brown as Capt. Oliver "Spearchucker" Jones
William Christopher as Father Francis Mulcahy
Odessa Cleveland as Lt. Ginger Bayliss

SYNOPSIS
When a rash of thefts run through the camp, Hawkeye is the prime suspect.

1. Which item of Frank's goes missing?

2. What is stolen from Hot Lips?

3. What item of Trapper's is stolen?

4. What does Hawkeye notice of his that has been stolen?

5. What falls on Henry's face when he is searching the Swamp's stovepipe?

6. Where are the missing items found?

7. Who is ordered to keep surveillance on Hawkeye?

8. Who is actually the one who has been stealing the items?

9. Why did he steal them?

EPISODE 1.11 "Germ Warfare"

Director: Terry Becker
Writer: Larry Gelbart

SELECTED SUPPORTING CAST
Odessa Cleveland as Lt. Ginger Bayliss
Patrick Adiarte as Ho-Jon
Timothy Brown as Capt. Oliver "Spearchucker" Jones
Bob Gooden as Pvt. Boone
Karen Philipp as Lt. Maria "Dish" Schneider
Byron Chung as POW

Other episodes with Byron Chung are "Iron Guts Kelly" (3.4), "Dear Ma" (4.16), "Out of Gas" (7.12), "The Yalu Brick Road" (8.10), "Communication Breakdown" (10.6), and "Foreign Affairs" (11.3).

SYNOPSIS
Chaos ensues when a blood shortage finds Hawkeye and Trapper tapping Frank in his sleep only to discover he may have hepatitis.

1. Which blood type is needed?

2. Where does the POW get billeted?

3. What does Hawkeye call Frank when he and Trapper think Frank has hepatitis?

4. Which nurse does Hawkeye tell Hot Lips is needed in Post Op?

5. What game are Frank and the POW playing in the Swamp during the last scene?

EPISODE 1.12 "Dear Dad"

Director: Gene Reynolds
Writer: Larry Gelbart

SELECTED SUPPORTING CAST
Jamie Farr as Cpl. Max Klinger
William Christopher as Father Francis Mulcahy
Odessa Cleveland as Lt. Ginger Bayliss
Bill Katt as PVC

Bill Katt may be more familiar to audiences as *William* Katt, who starred as reluctant superhero Ralph Hinkley in TV's *The Greatest American Hero*.

SYNOPSIS
Christmas at the 4077 finds Hawkeye writing a letter to his father about the goings-on in the camp.

1. Where does Hawkeye note his father being in the States?

2. What is Radar sending home?

3. What does Trapper throw to Hawkeye in the compound?

4. Who gives the Korean children their immunization shots?

5. What do the children get after their shot?

6. What does Frank take exception to Klinger wearing?

7. What does Mulcahy take from Klinger?

8. What does Hot Lips find in her pillow?

9. Who is slated to play Santa Claus for the kids?

10. How many soldiers are pinned down in the foxhole Hawkeye is sent to?

EPISODE 1.13 "Edwina"

Director: James Sheldon
Writer: Hal Dresner

SELECTED SUPPORTING CAST
Arlene Golonka as Lt. Edwina Ferguson
Marcia Strassman as Lt. Margie Cutler

Prior to her appearance on *MASH*, Arlene Golonka had portrayed Millie Hutchins on *The Andy Griffith Show* and Millie Swanson on *Mayberry R.F.D.*

SYNOPSIS
A klutzy nurse is in search of romance. Hawkeye draws the short straw.

1. What song does the staff sing that makes Edwina run from the mess tent crying?

2. Which condiment does Cutler ask for that causes a commotion when the men present try to beat each other in handing it to her?

3. What do the men do to determine who asks out Edwina?

4. According to Hawkeye, what is the mess tent coffee made from?

5. Who helps Hawkeye get dressed for his date?

6. What does Henry do when Hawkeye passes him on his way to Edwina?

7. Which color is Hawkeye's kimono?

EPISODE 1.14 "Love Story"

Director: Earl Bellamy
Writers: Larry Gelbart, Laurence Marks

SELECTED SUPPORTING CAST
Marcia Strassman as Lt. Margie Cutler
Kelly Jean Peters as Lt. Louise Anderson

SYNOPSIS
A lovesick Radar seeks romantic advice from Hawkeye.

1. How do Hawkeye and Trapper figure out something's upsetting Radar?

2. How many books does Hawkeye give to Radar?

3. What does Hawkeye tell Radar to say if the subject of Bach comes up?

4. Who has a problem with Radar trying to romance Lt. Anderson?

5. Who does Frank find together in Hot Lips' bed?

6. What does Trapper make Hot Lips say for her to give up trying to break up Radar and Anderson?

EPISODE 1.15 "Tuttle"

Director: William Wiard
Writer: Bruce Shelly, David Ketchum

SELECTED SUPPORTING CAST
Dennis Fimple as Sgt. "Sparky" Prior
Herb Voland as Brig. Gen. Clayton
Captain Tuttle as Himself

SYNOPSIS
What starts as Hawkeye's little white lie develops into a story even Hawkeye has trouble managing.

1. Who is afraid Tuttle will replace him?

2. What do Hawkeye and Trapper draw on Frank's photograph of McCarthy?

3. Where was Capt. Tuttle born?

4. What is Tuttle's hair color?

5. What does Trapper say when Hawkeye puts on the finishing touches to Tuttle's personnel file?

6. Who impersonates Gen. Clayton on the phone to Hot Lips?

7. Who is listening in to the phone conversation between Henry and Clayton?

8. What is the name of Tuttle's "replacement?"

EPISODE 1.16 "The Ringbanger"

Director: Jackie Cooper
Writer: Jerry Mayer

SELECTED SUPPORTING CAST
Leslie Nielsen as Col. Buzz Brighton

Director Cooper started as a child actor, the *Our Gang* shorts being perhaps the most famous of his youth, and later, younger audiences would know him as Perry White in the 1978 feature *Superman*.

The name Leslie Nielsen will cause memories of his considerable work, not the least of which being the film *Airplane!* (1980).

SYNOPSIS
It's up to Hawkeye and Trapper to keep an overly ambitious colonel off the front lines.

1. What does Hawkeye tell Buzz to do when he reaches the Swamp?

2. What does Buzz refuse to use in his recovery?

3. On which hand does Buzz wear his ring?

4. What was Buzz's all-time record for at West Point?

5. How many times do Hawkeye and Trapper "move" Buzz's quarters?

EPISODE 1.17 "Sometimes You Hear the Bullet"

Director: William Wiard
Writer: Carl Kleinschmitt

SELECTED SUPPORTING CAST
William Christopher as Fr. Francis Mulcahy
Ronny Howard as Wendell
James T. Callahan as Tommy Gillis

SYNOPSIS
An old friend of Hawkeye's shows up at the 4077.

Readers will obviously recognize the name Ronny Howard, who would later become Ron Howard. As an actor he would portray Richie Cunningham on TV's *Happy Days*, and would later transition *to* directing, helming such films as *Cocoon* and *Apollo 13*.

1. What song does Frank say gives him goosebumps?

2. What is Tommy Gillis' rank?

3. What does Tommy do when he meets Henry?

4. What is the name of the book Tommy is writing?

EPISODE 1.18 "Dear Dad... Again"

Director: Jackie Cooper
Writers: Sheldon Keller and Larry Gelbart

SELECTED SUPPORTING CAST
Jamie Farr as Cpl. Max Klinger
William Christopher as Fr. Francis Mulcahy
Odessa Cleveland as Lt. Ginger Bayliss
Alex Henteloff as Capt. Casey

SYNOPSIS
New surgeon Capt. Adam Casey is not what he seems.

1. What is Klinger wearing when he enters the Swamp with the x-rays?

2. Which tent does a naked Hawkeye walk into?

3. What test does Henry give Radar?

4. What does Frank ask Hawkeye and Trapper for after his fight with Margaret?

5. What does a drunk Frank say will happen if he closes his eyes?

6. What is "Captain" Casey's actual rank?

7. What is Casey's real last name?

EPISODE 1.19 "The Longjohn Flap"

Director: Adam Wiard
Writer: Alan Alda

SELECTED SUPPORTING CAST
Jamie Farr as Cpl. Max Klinger
William Christopher as Fr. Francis Mulcahy

SYNOPSIS
Winter in Korea finds a pair of longjohns going through a variety of owners.

1. What does Trapper break apart for firewood?

2. How does Trapper lose the longjohns?

3. What does Margaret use for mittens?

4. What happens to Henry after he gets the longjohns?

EPISODE 1.20 "The Army/Navy Game"

Director: Gene Reynolds
Writer: Sid Dorfman (teleplay), McLean Stevenson (story)

SELECTED SUPPORTING CAST
Jamie Farr as Cpl. Max Klinger
William Christopher as Fr. Francis Mulcahy

Season One • 31

SYNOPSIS
An unexploded bomb lands in the 4077 on the day of the Army/Navy football game.

1. What team does Mulcahy think is going to be playing?

2. Who does Henry think he's talking to on the phone following his injury?

3. Who draws the short match?

4. What does Frank do before he's supposed to check the bomb?

5. Who checks the bomb instead of Frank?

6. Who does the Army tell Henry to call about the bomb?

7. What was the score of Henry's Ohio State vs. Illinois football game?

8. What facial expression can Radar not do?

9. Who holds the toolbox when Hawkeye and Trapper try to defuse the bomb?

10. In which direction is Hawkeye instructed to turn the locking ring on the bomb?

11. What kind of bomb does it turn out to be?

EPISODE 1.21 "Sticky Wicket"

Director: Don Weis
Writer: Richard Baer

SELECTED SUPPORTING CAST
John Orchard as "Ugly" John

SYNOPSIS
Hawkeye and Frank lock horns over patients.

1. What is Radar drinking during the poker game?

2. What poker hand does Ugly John hold?

3. Where does Henry put his alarm clock?

4. Why does Hawkeye assault Frank?

5. Where does Hawkeye assault Frank?

6. What's in the box that's brought in to the tent Hawkeye stays in when away from the Swamp?

EPISODE 1.22 "Major Frank C. Dobbs"

Director: Don Weiss
Writer: Sid Dorfman

SELECTED SUPPORTING CAST
Odessa Cleveland as Lt. Ginger Bayliss

SYNOPSIS
A prank played on Frank and Hot Lips make them both demand transfers.

1. Who is the first person to think they've found gold?

2. According to Hot Lips, how does Frank like his pork chops?

3. What does Hawkeye say is his favorite military soap opera?

EPISODE 1.23 "Ceasefire"

Director: Earl Bellamy
Writer: Laurence Marks and Larry Gelbart (teleplay), Robert Klane (story)

SELECTED SUPPORTING CAST
Jamie Farr as Cpl. Max Klinger
William Christopher as Fr. Francis Mulcahy
Patrick Adiarte as Ho-Jon
Odessa Cleveland as Lt. Ginger Baker
Herb Voland as Gen. Crandell Clayton

SYNOPSIS
The 4077 celebrates a ceasefire that may lead to the end the war, but Trapper has his doubts.

1. Who tells Henry about the ceasefire?

2. What does the staff use as streamers?

3. What does Trapper write in Radar's memory book?

4. What do Frank and Margaret do during the ceasefire?

EPISODE 1.24 "Showtime"

Director: Jackie Cooper
Writer: Larry Gelbart

SELECTED SUPPORTING CAST
Joey Forman as Jackie Flash
William Christopher as Fr. Francis Mulcahy
Harvey J. Goldenberg as Dr. Kaplan
Marilyn King, Jean Turrell, and Joan Lucksinger as The
    Miller Sisters

You may be able to find Don Most (*Happy Days*'s Ralph Malph) in an uncredited role as a wounded soldier.

SYNOPSIS
The USO visits the 4077.

1. What are Hawkeye and Trapper doing during the USO show?

2. What happens when the still malfunctions?

3. What was Henry's sympathy pregnancy craving?

4. Who performs a drum solo with the band?

SEASON TWO

STARRING

Alan Alda as Capt. Benjamin Franklin "Hawkeye" Pierce

Wayne Rogers as Capt. "Trapper" John McIntyre

McLean Stevenson as Lt. Col. Henry Blake

Loretta Swit as Maj. Margaret "Hot Lips" Houlihan

Larry Linville as Maj. Frank Burns

Gary Burghoff as Cpl. Walter "Radar" O'Reilly

Jamie Farr as Cpl. Max Klinger

William Christopher as Fr. Francis Mulcahy

Trivia answers for Season Two begin on page 276.

EPISODE 2.1 "Divided We Stand"

Director: Jackie Cooper
Written by: Larry Gelbart

SELECTED SUPPORTING CAST:
Anthony Holland as Capt. Hildebrand
Herb Voland as Gen. Crandell Clayton
Odessa Cleveland as Lt. Ginger Bayliss

SYNOPSIS
Gen. Clayton sends a psychiatrist to the 4077 to review the staff.

1. What does Clayton call Hot Lips?

2. What does Radar bring in to Henry and Hildebrand?

3. Where does Henry hold his secret meeting?

4. What is said to be in Frank's boot?

5. What is Hawkeye doing in Henry's office during the meeting with Hildebrand?

6. What is the skeleton wearing around its neck?

EPISODE 2.2 "Five O'Clock Charlie"

Director: Norman Tokar
Written by: Larry Gelbart, Laurence Marks and Keith
    Walker (teleplay), Keith Walker (story)

SELECTED SUPPORTING CAST:
Herb Voland as Gen. Crandell Clayton
Odessa Cleveland as Lt. Ginger Bayliss
Sarah Fankboner as Lt. Klein, RN

SYNOPSIS
The staff bets on the accuracy of a "washout from Kamikaze school," much to Frank and Hot Lips' displeasure.

1. How many weeks has Charlie been trying to bomb the 4077?

2. What weapon does Frank want?

3. What makes Gen. Clayton decide to give the 4077 the anti-aircraft gun?

4. How many men does Frank recruit as a gun crew?

5. What is Hawkeye holding instead of a rifle when hassling Frank?

6. How many sheets do Hawkeye and Trapper get from Lt. Klein?

7. How are Hawkeye and Trapper drinking martinis in the shower?

8. How many explosions go off when Charlie hits the ammo dump?

9. Which newspaper is Frank reading when the walls of the latrine collapse?

EPISODE 2.3 "Radar's Report"

Director: Jackie Cooper
Written by: Laurence Marks (teleplay), Sheldon Keller (story)

SELECTED SUPPORTING CAST:
Allan Arbus as Maj. Milton Freedman (later to be *Sidney* Freedman)
Joan Van Ark as Lt. Erica Johnson

Joan Van Ark would later go on to appear on TV's *Dallas*, and its spin-off, *Knots Landing*.

SYNOPSIS
The highlights from one of Radar's weekly reports.

1. What does a bleary-eyed Radar accidentally start typing on instead of his typewriter?

2. Which blood type does Trapper's patient need?

3. Who was in Hot Lips' tent using the hair dryer when Frank came in?

4. What is the skeleton in Henry's office wearing around its neck?

5. What does Radar pretend to feed his teddy bear?

6. What's the first thing Dr. Freedman asks Klinger?

7. Who tells Trapper his patient has died?

8. What is Henry doing in the last scene when Radar enters his office?

EPISODE 2.4 "For the Good of the Outfit"

Director: Jackie Cooper
Written by: Jerry Mayer

SELECTED SUPPORTING CAST:
Odessa Cleveland as Lt Ginger Bayliss
Frank Aletter as Maj. Stoner
Herb Voland as Gen. Crandell Clayton

SYNOPSIS
Hawkeye and Trapper discover the US military is responsible for the shelling of a civilian village.

1. How American does Trapper call the shrapnel removed from the villagers?

2. Who does Hawkeye and Trapper ask to also sign the report?

3. Why does Radar think Maj. Stoner is in camp on serious business?

4. What does Henry do before meeting with Gen. Clayton?

EPISODE 2.5 "Dr. Pierce and Mr. Hyde"

Director: Jackie Cooper
Written by: Alan Alda and Robert Klane

SELECTED SUPPORTING CAST:
Buck Young as O'Brien
Herb Voland as Gen. Crandell Clayton

SYNOPSIS
An exhausted Hawkeye begins to show erratic behavior.

1. What sound do Trapper and Hawkeye hope the sound of approaching helicopter rotors is?

2. According to Trapper, how many hours has Hawkeye been in the OR?

3. What does Radar use to get Hawkeye to the Swamp?

4. What does Hawkeye walk into without realizing it?

5. What is Radar doing when Hawkeye goes to his office after he talks to Trapper?

6. What two-word question does Hawkeye ask President Truman in his telegram?

7. Who is giving an orientation lecture in the mess tent to the enlisted men?

8. What is Hawkeye taking a picture of after he talks to Frank during the lecture?

EPISODE 2.6 "Kim"

Director: William Wiard
Written by: Marc Mandel, Larry Gelbart and Laurence Marks

SELECTED SUPPORTING CAST:
Maggie Roswell as Sister Theresa
Edgar Miller as Kim

SYNOPSIS
Trapper tries to adopt what is believed to be an orphaned five-year-old boy.

1. Who orders Trapper and Hawkeye to leave Kim alone?

2. What does Klinger play with Kim?

3. What does Radar take away from Kim as they both are sleeping?

4. What children's story is Hot Lips reading to Kim?

5. What letter does Radar file the map to the minefield under and why?

6. What is the name of the chopper pilot who rescues Trapper and Kim?

7. Who does O'Brien pick up first?

EPISODE 2.7 "LIP (Local Indigenous Personnel)"

Director: William Wiard
Written by: Carl Kleinschmitt, Larry Gelbart and Laurence Marks

SELECTED SUPPORTING CAST:
Burt Young as Lt. Willis
Corrine Camacho as Lt. Regina Hopkins

SYNOPSIS
Hawkeye and Trapper help a soldier headed home to marry a Korean woman and take her to the States.

1. Where is Hawkeye's date with Regina?

2. Who is the star in the unnamed movie they're waiting for?

3. Who ends up having dinner with Regina instead?

4. On whose cot does Lt. Willis pass out on?

5. What do Trapper and Hawkeye try to do to Lt. Willis to get him to help them?

6. Who catches the bouquet in the last scene?

EPISODE 2.8 "The Trial of Henry Blake"

Director: Don Weis
Written by: McLean Stevenson

SELECTED SUPPORTING CAST:
Robert F. Simon as Gen. Maynard M. Mitchell
Hope Summers as Nurse Meg Cratty

SYNOPSIS
Hot Lips and Frank file formal charges against Henry's command.

1. What game are Hawkeye and Trapper playing when Henry departs with Radar?

2. Whose product is Radar selling?

3. Who is the first person he tries to sell to?

4. What does Klinger build to get out of camp?

5. Upon witnessing Klinger's attempt, how do both Hawkeye and Trapper describe the sight?

6. How many MPs guard Hawkeye and Trapper in the Swamp?

EPISODE 2.9 "Dear Dad... Three"

Director: Don Weis
Written by: Laurence Marks and Larry Gelbart

SELECTED SUPPORTING CAST:
Mills Watson as Sgt. Condon
Kathleen Hughes as Lorraine Blake
Odessa Cleveland as Lt. Ginger Bayliss

SYNOPSIS
Hawkeye keeps his father up-to-date on the goings-on at the 4077.

1. What game are Trapper and Frank playing?

2. Who assists Hawkeye and Henry with the live grenade?

3. How did Frank's wife "trick" him into marriage?

4. What is Frank's middle name?

5. Who climbs onto the table at the end of the staff meeting?

EPISODE 2.10 "The Sniper"

Director: Jackie Cooper
Written by: Richard M. Powell

SELECTED SUPPORTING CAST:
Teri Garr as Lt. Suzanne Marquette
Dennis Troy as Ambulance Driver

Teri Garr is known for her roles in *Young Frankenstein*, *Close Encounters of the Third Kind*, and *Tootsie*, among others.

SYNOPSIS
A sniper has the staff at the 4077 pinned down.

1. What's special about Frank's pistol?

2. Where are Radar and Henry pinned down?

3. How many times does the sniper shoot at Radar?

4. Who quiets the staff down for Frank to speak?

5. How do Henry and Radar manage to escape the showers?

6. According to the driver, how many wounded are in the ambulance?

7. Where was the driver shot?

8. Who holds the white flag when the staff gets the wounded from the ambulance?

9. How long does Frank admit it took him to complete med school?

10. Where does Frank and Hawkeye think the sniper is lurking?

11. How does a frustrated Henry hang up the phone in his office?

12. What does Hawkeye use to help him get up the hill to the wounded sniper?

EPISODE 2.11 "Carry On, Hawkeye"

Director: Jackie Cooper
Written by: Bernard Dilbert, Larry Gelbart and Laurence Marks (teleplay), Bernard Gilbert (story)

SELECTED SUPPORTING CAST:
Marcia Gelman as Lt. Jacobs
Gwen Farrell as Lt. Wilson

SYNOPSIS
Hawkeye is left as the lone able surgeon when the flu hits the camp.

1. Who is the first of the doctors to go down with the flu?

2. What does Hot Lips retrieve from the Swamp on Frank's behalf?

3. Complete Hawkeye's cry of frustration in OR. "My kingdom for an…?"

4. What does a feverish Henry call Hot Lips and Hawkeye when he finds them in his office?

5. A delirious Frank mistakes Hot Lips for whom?

EPISODE 2.12 "The Incubator"

Director: Jackie Cooper
Written by: Larry Gelbart and Laurence Marks

SELECTED SUPPORTING CAST:
Robert F. Simon as Gen. Maynard M. Mitchell
Ted Gehring as Maj. Arnold Morris
Logan Ramsey as Col. Lambert
Eldon Quick as Capt. Sloan

SYNOPSIS

The misadventures of Trapper and Hawkeye as they try to get the 4077 an incubator.

1. In the opening scene in the Swamp, what object is turning on the record player?

2. What does Radar bring to the Swamp for Hawkeye and Trapper?

3. What unusual item does Trapper wear when making his morning rounds in Post Op?

4. According to Henry, how many people managed to fit in one sleeping bag at the Swamp's party?

5. What does Radar ask Hawkeye and Trapper if the incubator can do?

EPISODE 2.13 "Deal Me Out"

Director: Gene Reynolds
Written by: Larry Gelbart and Laurence Marks

SELECTED SUPPORTING CAST:
Pat Morita as Capt. Sam Pak
Allan Arbus as Maj. Sidney Freedman (formerly Milton Freedman)
Edward Winter as Capt. Halloran
John Ritter as Pvt. Carter
Jerry Fujikawa as "Whiplash" Wang
Tom Dever as Lt. Rogers

Pat Morita is best known as Mr. Miyagi in the original *Karate Kid* movies and as Matsuo "Arnold" Takahashi on *Happy Days*.

Allan Arbus's work included appearances on various TV programs, from *Starsky and Hutch* to *Curb Your Enthusiasm*. John Ritter would go on to star in TV's *Three's Company* and feature films such as the acclaimed *Sling Blade*.

Jerry Fujikawa's work on *MASH* would include other appearances in "The Chosen People" (2.19), "Officer of the Day" (3.3), "Love and Marriage" (3.20), "Rally 'Round the Flagg, Boys" (7.21), "Back Pay" (8.24), and "The Birthday Girls" (10.11).

Tom Dever would appear in the episodes "Aid Station" (3.19), "Welcome to Korea" (4.1), "Change Day" (6.0), and "They Call the Wind Korea" (7.7).

SYNOPSIS
A poker game is interrupted by a series of mishaps.

1. Who is the first visitor to arrive at the camp?

2. When does the "conference" start?

3. How does Radar retaliate against Hawkeye and Trapper in the showers?

4. Which two colors are in Klinger's hat?

5. At the game, why does Hawkeye warn everyone not to move?

6. Who does Sam say Klinger is when questioned by Halloran?

7. What condition does Sidney demand before going out where the shooting is?

8. Where is Frank held hostage by Pvt. Carter?

9. Who apprehends Carter?

EPISODE 2.14 "Hot Lips and Empty Arms"

Director: Jackie Cooper
Written by: Linda Bloodworth and Mary Kay Place

SELECTED SUPPORTING CAST:
Kellye Nakahara as Lt. Kellye Yamato

SYNOPSIS
Hot Lips decides that it's time for a change in her life and requests a transfer.

1. What does Hot Lips return to Frank?

2. What does Hot Lips want from Henry when she visits him in his office?

3. What do they drink?

4. By what name does the drunken Hot Lips call Henry?

5. Who does she confess an attraction to?

6. What kind of shot does Hawkeye give her?

EPISODE 2.15 "Officers Only"

Director: Jackie Cooper
Written by: Ed Jurist

SELECTED SUPPORTING CAST:
Robert F. Simon as Gen. Maynard M. Mitchell
Robert Weaver as Pvt. Gary Mitchell
Odessa Cleveland as Lt. Ginger Bayliss
Clyde Kusatsu as Kwang Duk

Clyde Kusatsu would appear in "Henry in Love" (2.26), "Goodbye Cruel World" (8.21), and "The Joker's Wild" (11.4).

SYNOPSIS
After they treat his son's wounds, Gen. Mitchell gives the camp its own Officer's Club.

1. Who wakes up Hawkeye?

2. What kind of condition does Klinger claim to be in?

3. What did Hawkeye and Trapper allegedly send to Gen. MacArthur's table?

4. What unusual thing do the enlisted men do when Hawkeye and Trapper enter the mess tent?

5. What does Henry say they can use the jukebox for if they throw a tarp over it?

6. What drink does Frank order?

7. Which number is on Trapper's basketball jersey?

EPISODE 2.16 "Henry in Love"

Director: Don Weis
Written by: Larry Gelbart and Laurence Marks

SELECTED SUPPORTING CAST:
Kathrine Baumann as Nancy Sue Parker
Kellye Nakahara as Kellye Yamato

SYNOPSIS
Henry falls for a woman less than half his age.

1. What is Frank drinking in Hot Lips' tent?

2. What color are the border rocks around the Swamp in this particular episode?

3. What does Henry say he's beginning to brush his hair with?

4. What of Henry's does Hawkeye say is bleeding?

5. Who says, "It's nice to be nice to the nice"?

6. What interrupts the punchline to the joke Hawkeye tells outside the Officers' Club?

7. What does Henry's son hit his sister with?

EPISODE 2.17 "For Want of a Boot"

Director: Don Weis
Written by: Sheldon Keller
SELECTED SUPPORTING CAST:
Michael Lerner as Capt. Futterman
Johnny Haymer as Sgt. Zelmo Zale

SYNOPSIS
Hawkeye must go to ridiculous lengths to get a new pair of boots.

1. What does Radar tell Hawkeye the camp is receiving?

2. What does Hawkeye use to patch the hole in his boot?

3. What does Hot Lips want Hawkeye to do for Frank?

4. What gift does Hot Lips give to Frank?

5. In the last scene, what is Hawkeye using as a replacement boot?

EPISODE 2.18 "Operation Noselift"

Director: Hy Averback
Written by: Erik Tarloff (teleplay), Paul Richards and Erik Tarloff (story)

SELECTED SUPPORTING CAST:
Todd Susman as Pvt. Danny Baker
Stuart Margolin as Maj. Stanley Robbins

SYNOPSIS
A soldier wants Hawkeye and Trapper to help him get a nose job.

1. What does Henry say he's not good at?

2. What is Hawkeye's nickname for Maj. Robbins?

3. Who fakes a broken nose to cover for Pvt. Baker?

4. Where does Trapper check for Maj. Robinson?

EPISODE 2.19 "The Chosen People"

Director: Jackie Cooper
Written by: Laurence Marks, Sheldon Keller and Larry Gelbart (teleplay), Gerry Renert and Jeff Wilhelm (story)

SELECTED SUPPORTING CAST:
Pat Morita as Capt. Sam Pak
Clare Nono as Choon-Hi
Jerry Fujikawa as Father

SYNOPSIS
A Korean family moves into the compound. One of the staff may be the father of a Korean woman's baby.

1. What is thrown at Radar as he plays "Reveille"?

2. What does Capt. Pak say is his father-in-law's name?

3. What does Radar say when he sees the cow in Henry's tent?

4. What does Frank suggest the camp do to clear the family out?

5. Who does Choon-Hi claim to be the father of her baby?

6. How many MPs does Frank take along to remove the family?

EPISODE 2.20 "As You Were"

Director: Hy Averback
Written by: Larry Gelbart and Laurence Marks (teleplay), Gene Reynolds (story)

SELECTED SUPPORTING CAST:
Kellye Nakahara as Lt. Kellye Yamato

SYNOPSIS
Boredom in the camp during lulls; chaos when the war gets back into full swing.

1. Who is playing piano in the O Club?

2. What's Mulcahy doing when Klinger visits his tent?

3. What do Trapper and Hawkeye put Frank in while he sleeps?

4. What are in the packages delivered to Hawkeye and Trapper?

5. What aspect of Henry does Trapper compliment him on in the OR?

6. How many ranks does Radar impersonate over the phone trying to get the shelling stopped?

EPISODE 2.21 "Crisis"

Director: Don Weis
Written by: Larry Gelbart and Laurence Marks

SYNOPSIS
The camp struggles when its supply line is cut.

1. What condition does Hot Lips suggest the camp be under during the crisis?

2. What game is Mulcahy hosting?

3. What does Frank bring to Hot Lips?

4. Who interrupts Mulcahy's prayer?

5. Which article of clothing is pinned to the bulletin board?

6. Who tries to sleep in the nurses' tent?

7. At the end of the episode, what are the only two things left in Henry's office?

EPISODE 2.22 "George"

Director: Gene Reynolds
Written by: John W. Regier and Gary Markowitz

SELECTED SUPPORTING CAST:
Richard Ely as Pvt. George Weston

SYNOPSIS
A highly decorated soldier is beaten by men in his own unit for being gay.

1. Which song is Trapper singing in the OR?

2. What does Trapper do when Frank complains about the singing?

3. Who is tackled by a number of staffers during a football game?

4. What game are Hawkeye and Trapper playing in the Swamp?

5. Which part of Frank does Hawkeye want to quarantine?

6. What does Radar say he sees in Henry's ear?

EPISODE 2.23 "Mail Call"

Director: Alan Alda
Written by: Larry Gelbart and Laurence Marks

SELECTED SUPPORTING CAST:
Sheila Lauritsen as Nurse Sheila
Kellye Nakahara as Lt. Kellye Yamamoto

SYNOPSIS
The staff receive some much-needed mail from home.

1. What does Hawkeye's sister send him?

2. What does Henry's wife want him to do for her?

3. How can Hot Lips tell when Frank is double-talking?

4. What is the name of the fictional stock Frank wants to invest in?

5. Who is playing piano in the O Club?

6. What two words does Hot Lip yell repeatedly after Frank upsets her?

7. What does Hawkeye pretend to knight Radar with?

8. What time does Hot Lips tell Frank to be at her tent to make up to her?

EPISODE 2.24 "A Smattering of Intelligence"

Director: Larry Gelbart
Written by: Larry Gelbart and Laurence Marks

SELECTED SUPPORTING CAST:
Edward Winter as Col. Samuel Flagg (previously Capt. Halloran. Flagg has many aliases)
Bill Fletcher as Vinnie Pratt

SYNOPSIS
There is a suspected intelligence leak coming from the camp.

1. What is Hawkeye chewing on while examining Col. Flagg?

2. How many aliases does Flagg show to Henry?

3. How many times does Flagg's arm get broken?

4. What does Col. Flagg use to break his arm the second time?

5. What is Pratt's code name?

6. What does Radar do to signal Hawkeye?

SEASON THREE

STARRING

Alan Alda as Capt. Benjamin Franklin "Hawkeye" Pierce

Wayne Rogers as Capt. "Trapper" John McIntyre

McLean Stevenson as Lt. Col. Henry Blake

Loretta Swit as Maj. Margaret "Hot Lips" Houlihan*

Larry Linville as Maj. Frank Burns

Gary Burghoff as Cpl. Walter "Radar" O'Reilly

Jamie Farr as Cpl. Max Klinger

William Christopher as Fr. Francis Mulcahy

---

*As noted in the introduction, as the character of Maj. Houlihan progressed, she became referred to by her nickname less and less. It is in this season that we acknowledge this, calling her by her first name, Margaret.

Trivia answers for Season Three begin on page 284.

EPISODE 3.1 "The General Flipped at Dawn"

Director: Larry Gelbart
Written by: Jim Fritzell and Everett Greenbaum

SELECTED SUPPORTING CAST:
Harry Morgan as Maj. Gen. Bartford Hamilton Steele
Theodore Wilson as Warrant Officer Martin "Marty" Williams

Harry Morgan would, in his storied career, also appear as Col. Sherman T. Potter in the fourth season of *MASH*.

SYNOPSIS

A visiting general's behavior goes from eccentric to insane.

1. Where is the model boat race being held?

2. Who does Trapper say shot John Wilkes Booth?

3. Which three staffers get out of the ambulance at the helipad?

4. By what collective nickname does Hawkeye refer to himself and Trapper?

5. How many stars does Gen. Steele have in his rank?

6. What does Gen. Steele tell Frank to trim?

7. What is Maj. Steele's wife's name?

8. While doing rounds in Post-Op, where does Hawkeye store his sandwich?

9. What instrument does Trapper play in this episode?

10. How many minutes away is the front from the 4077?

EPISODE 3.2 "Rainbow Bridge"

Director: Hy Averback
Written by: Larry Gelbart and Laurence Marks

SELECTED SUPPORTING CAST:
Mako as Dr. Lin Tam
Loudon Wainwright III as Capt. Calvin Spalding

Mako will be recognizable from his considerable amount of work in film and TV—including the additional *MASH* episodes "Hawkeye Get Your Gun" (5.10), "Guerilla My Dreams" (8.3) and "The Best of Enemies" (9.1)—from 1955 to posthumous work in 2007 (having passed away in 2006).

Loudon Wainwright III was an actor and musician working in three *MASH* episodes in addition to TV and film work. His son, Rufus Wainwright, is a successful musician in his own right.

SYNOPSIS
Henry tries to broker a prisoner exchange with Chinese forces.

1. Who is seen giving Hawkeye a manicure?

2. Who does Mulcahy smack in the face with the door as he exits the Swamp?

3. How many American GIs do the Chinese have to exchange?

4. How many miles behind enemy lines is the exchange to take place?

5. Who gives Frank a gun to take to the exchange?

6. How many staffers from the 4077 go to the exchange?

7. What kind of damaged vehicle does the MASH bus stop near?

8. What does Dr. Tam say when he sees Frank's gun?

EPISODE 3.3 "Officer of the Day"

Director: Hy Averback
Written by: Laurence Marks

SELECTED SUPPORTING CAST:
Edward Winter as Col. Samuel Flagg

Jeff Maxwell as Pvt. Igor Straminsky
Dennis Troy as Carter
Richard Lee-Sung as 2nd Korean Kim Luk

Other episodes with Richard Lee-Sung would be "Dear Mildred" (4.7), "Some 38th Parallels"(4.19), "Bug Out" (5.1), "Change Day" (6.8), "The MASH Olympics" (6.10), "The Smell of Music" (6.15), "A Night At Rosie's" (7.23), "Goodbye, Radar.Part 1" (8.4), "Snap Judgement" (10.7), and "That Darn Kid" (10.21).

SYNOPSIS

Col. Flagg comes to the camp on the day Hawkeye is assigned Officer of the Day duty.

1. Who fires the cannon during morning inspection?

2. What does Hawkeye tell Frank he refuses to carry?

3. What does Hawkeye tell the sentries to keep handy?

4. What does Hawkeye claim "OD" stands for?

5. What does Trapper put in his shirt pocket in the scrub room?

6. Who doubles for the North Korean prisoner?

7. How many LIPs named Kim Luk does Hawkeye see in total?

8. What's wrong with Trapper's pinstripe suit?

EPISODE 3.4 "Iron Guts Kelly"

Director: Don Weis
Written by: Larry Gelbart and Sid Dorfman

SELECTED SUPPORTING CAST:
James Gregory as Gen. Robert "Iron Guts" Kelly
Keene Curtis as Col. Wortman
Byron Chung as Mr. Kwok
Jeff Maxwell as Pvt. Igor Straminsky

SYNOPSIS
A legendary general dies in Margaret's tent.

1. What gets stuck to one of the fishing lures on Henry's hat?

2. How many stars does Gen. Kelly have?

3. Who do Hawkeye and Trapper see on their way to help at Margaret's tent?

4. What is Col. Wortman doing when Hawkeye and Trapper tell him about Kelly?

5. What does Frank accidentally sit on in Margaret's tent?

EPISODE 3.5 "O.R."

Director: Gene Reynolds
Written by: Larry Gelbart and Laurence Marks

SELECTED SUPPORTING CAST:
Bobbie Mitchell as Lt. Able
Odessa Cleveland as Lt. Ginger Bayliss
Orlando Dolé as Ethiopian Soldier

SYNOPSIS
The staff must deal with a heavy influx of wounded.

1. Which item of Frank's goes missing?

2. From which country is the wounded man who kisses Hawkeye's hand?

3. What movie's audio is being piped into OR?

4. Who stops Frank from taking a kidney from a patient?

5. Who impersonates Dracula when they are told they must give blood?

6. What does Radar bring in to the OR for the surgeons to drink?

7. Who puts out the fire in OR?

EPISODE 3.6 "Springtime"

Director: Don Weis
Written by: Linda Bloodworth and Mary Kay Place

SELECTED SUPPORTING CAST:
Alex Karras as Lance Cpl. Lyle Wesson
Mary Kay Place as Lt. Louise Simmons
Gwen Farrell as Lt. Baker

Alex Karras played defensive tackle for the Detroit Lions, and would continue to act in film and TV such as *Blazing Saddles* and *Webster*.

Mary Kay Place, co-writer of the script, co-starred in this episode. She went on to write and direct for a variety of TV shows and act in numerous features such as *The Big Chill* and *Being John Malkovich*.

SYNOPSIS
The spring brings with it wishes of romance amongst the staff.

1. Who interrupts Henry's golf swing?

2. Who gets the cat away from the soldier?

3. What is Klinger wearing for his wedding?

EPISODE 3.7 "Check-Up"

Director: Don Weis
Written by: Laurence Marks

SELECTED SUPPORTING CAST:
Patricia Stevens as Lt. Stevens

SYNOPSIS
Trapper's ulcer may be his ticket home.

1. What does Trapper pour into his martini glass?

2. Who gives Margaret her physical?

3. What tattoo does Radar have?

4. Who tries to give Trapper his physical?

5. What city does Trapper say his ulcer could light up?

6. What does Radar ask when Henry tells him to get some milk?

7. Who's dancing with Kellye in the O Club?

8. Which song can Frank play on the spoons?

EPISODE 3.8 "Life with Father"

Director: Hy Averback
Written by: Everett Greenbaum and Jim Fritzell

SELECTED SUPPORTING CAST:
Sachiko Penny Lee as Chim Sa

SYNOPSIS
A Korean woman is looking for a rabbi for her baby's bris.

1. What is Trapper doing when Henry reads his letter from home to him and Hawkeye?

2. On which naval aircraft carrier does Radar find a rabbi?

3. What lab instrument do Trapper and Hawkeye use to search the puzzle they're working on?

4. What does Henry do to himself to prove he doesn't cry?

EPISODE 3.9 "Alcoholics Unanimous"

Director: Hy Averback
Written by: Everett Greenbaum and Jim Fritzell

SELECTED SUPPORTING CAST:
Jeff Maxwell as Pvt. Igor Straminsky
Kellye Nakahara as Lt. Kellye Yamato

SYNOPSIS
While Henry's away, acting CO Frank outlaws alcohol on the base.

1. Who does Frank order to take down the still?

2. Who does Mulcahy say is the only one who ever attends Sunday services?

3. What does Margaret tell Frank she keeps in her hip flask?

4. What is the book and chapter of the Bible Mulcahy reads?

5. What does a drunk Mulcahy ask Radar to open?

EPISODE 3.10 "There's Nothing Like a Nurse"

Director: Hy Averback
Written by: Larry Gelbart

SELECTED SUPPORTING CAST:
Loudon Wainwright III as Capt. Calvin Spalding
Jeanne Schulherr as Louise Burns

SYNOPSIS
The nurses are evacuated when there's a fear of the camp being overrun by the enemy.

1. What condition is Henry in when Margaret comes into his office?

2. Who informs Trapper, Hawkeye, and Spalding why the nurses are leaving?

3. By how many feet does Hawkeye tell Radar people in camp are unhappier than he is?

4. What does Frank give to Margaret to remember him by?

5. How do Trapper and Hawkeye trap Frank in a foxhole?

EPISODE 3.11 "Adam's Ribs"

Director: Gene Reynolds
Written by: Laurence Marks
SELECTED SUPPORTING CAST:
Joseph Stern as Master Sgt. Tarola
Basil Hoffman as Maj. Pfiefer

SYNOPSIS
Hawkeye sends out for barbeque ribs… from Chicago.

1. Which two mess tent foods is Hawkeye sick of?

2. Who keeps eating during Hawkeye's "We want something else" rant?

3. How many pounds of ribs and gallons of sauce does Hawkeye order?

4. What does Hawkeye forget to order?

EPISODE 3.12 "A Full Rich Day"

Director: Gene Reynolds
Written by: John D. Hess

SELECTED SUPPORTING CAST:
Curt Lowens as Col. Blanche
Kellye Nakahara as Lt. Kellye Yamato
Sirri Murad as Turkish Soldier with Knife

Sirri Murad would also appear in "Captains Outrageous" (8.13).

SYNOPSIS
Hawkeye tape records a letter to his dad.

1. Which soldier does the camp lose?

2. From where does the nickname "Hawkeye" come from?

3. Which soldier attacks Henry?

4. How does Hawkeye refer to Trapper in his tape?

5. Whose clothes does the Turk wear when returning to the front?

6. What does the Turkish soldier call Hawkeye?

EPISODE 3.13 "Mad Dogs and Servicemen"

Director: Hy Averback
Written by: Linda Bloodworth and Mary Kay Place

SELECTED SUPPORTING CAST:
Michael O'Keefe as Cpl. Richard Travis
Shizuko Hoshi as Rosie

The role of Rosie would have a few actresses playing the role. Shizuko Hoshi, who was married in real-life to actor Mako, would also be seen in the episodes "Hawkeye" (4.18), "BJ Papa San" (7.15), and "Private Finance" (8.8).

SYNOPSIS
Radar gets bitten by a dog that may be rabid.

1. What animal does Henry return to Radar?

2. Who helps Radar look for the dog?

3. Which city does Trapper say he interned in?

EPISODE 3.14 "Private Charles Lamb"

Director: Hy Averback
Written by: Sid Dorfman

SELECTED SUPPORTING CAST:
Titos Vandis as Col. Andropolis
Ted Eccles as Pvt. Chapman

SYNOPSIS
Easter comes to the 4077 with the help of the Greek Army.

1. Which animal does Radar take out of its cage?

2. How many cats does Radar have at home?

3. What did the draft board have to remove from Radar's throat?

4. What is Hawkeye chewing on when he relieves Trapper in Post Op?

5. What is Henry repairing when Frank visits him in his office?

6. Who falls down while swaying/dancing with Hawkeye and the Greek soldiers?

EPISODE 3.15 "Bombed"

Director: Hy Averback
Written by: Jim Fritzell and Everett Greenbaum

SELECTED SUPPORTING CAST:
Louisa Moritz as Nurse Sanchez

SYNOPSIS
Friendly artillery fire threatens the camp.

1. Who, besides Henry, was in the latrine when it was hit?

2. What does Lt. Sanchez do when Margaret slaps her?

3. Who notices the shelling has stopped?

4. Who asks, "No more boom-boom?"

EPISODE 3.16 "Bulletin Board"

Director: Alan Alda
Written by: Larry Gelbart and Simon Muntner

SELECTED SUPPORTING CAST:
Johnny Haymer as Sgt. Zelmo Zale
Kellye Nakahara as Lt. Charlie

SYNOPSIS
The 4077 throws a benefit for the local orphans.

1. What does Trapper pretend to do during Henry's lecture?

2. What does Hawkeye say to Frank during the lecture?

3. What does Hawkeye throw at Trapper when Trapper wakes him up?

4. Who is the star of the movie being watched in the mess tent?

5. What does Margaret do when Frank gives her a balloon?

6. What does Margaret do when Frank mentions the condition of the loan he'll give her?

EPISODE 3.17 "The Consultant"

Director: Gene Reynolds
Written by: Robert Klane (teleplay), Larry Gelbart (story)

SELECTED SUPPORTING CAST:
Robert Alda as Dr. Anthony Borelli

Robert Alda (father to Alan) made his film debut as George Gershwin in *Rhapsody in Blue* and originated the role of Sky Masterson on Broadway in *Guys and Dolls*.

SYNOPSIS
Hawkeye and Trapper meet a doctor in a Tokyo bar and are surprised when he shows up at the 4077.

1. What drink at the Tokyo bar does Trapper order?

2. To which war does Hawkeye propose a toast?

3. Which county's army supplies the arterial transplant?

4. Which two people does Hawkeye say he's going to stitch together?

EPISODE 3.18 "House Arrest"

Director: Hy Averback
Written by: Jim Fritzell and Everett Greenbaum

SELECTED SUPPORTING CAST:
Kellye Nakahara as Lt. Kellye Yamato
Dennis Troy as MP
Bobbie Mitchell as Lt. Baker

SYNOPSIS
Hawkeye is put under house arrest for assaulting Frank.

1. What does Frank do to Hawkeye that makes Hawkeye deck Frank?

2. In his report, what does Trapper say Frank slipped on rather than having been hit by Hawkeye?

3. What does Fr. Mulcahy bring to Hawkeye?

4. What does Frank think makes Radar look different?

5. How many MPs escort Hawkeye to the latrine?

EPISODE 3.19 "Aid Station"

Director: William Jurgensen
Written by: Larry Gelbart and Simon Muntner

SELECTED SUPPORTING CAST:
Tom Dever as Corpsman

SYNOPSIS
Hawkeye, Margaret, and Klinger must go help at an aid station at the front.

1. Who is the first to volunteer?

2. What does Hawkeye do to his aftershave bottles before he leaves?

3. Who almost gets hit by flying martini glasses?

4. Who changes the tire on the jeep?

5. What is Radar's radio callsign?

6. Which song does Frank hum while flossing?

7. What song do Margaret, Hawkeye, and Klinger sing as they near the 4077?

EPISODE 3.20 "Love and Marriage"

Director: Lee Philips
Written by: Arthur Julian

SELECTED SUPPORTING CAST:
Dennis Dugan as Pvt. Danny McShane
Johnny Haymer as Sgt. Zelmo Zale
Soon-Taik Oh as Mr. Kwang

Dennis Dugan would also appear in "Strange Bedfellows" (11.11) and would go on to portray Richie Brockelman from *The Rockford Files*, and its spinoff, *Richie Brockelman, Private Eye*.

Soon-Taik Oh (aka Soon-Tek Oh) would act in episodes "The Bus" (4.6), "The Korean Surgeon" (5.9), "The Yalu Brick Road" (8.10), and "Foreign Affairs" (11.3).

SYNOPSIS
A private in the US Army wants to marry a Korean woman, but Hawkeye and Trapper have their suspicions.

1. Who do Trapper and Hawkeye ask to help get them a three-day pass for Mr. Kwang?

2. What unusual item of Hawkeye's does Radar eat at the poker game?

3. How many warning shots does Frank fire when Mr. Kwan flees?

4. Where does Trapper say Dr. Pak received his medical diploma?

5. What does Radar volunteer to go find when Mrs. Kwan goes into labor on the bus?

EPISODE 3.21 "Big Mac"

Director: Don Weis
Written by: Laurence Marks

SELECTED SUPPORTING CAST:
Graham Jarvis as Col. Whiteman
Loudon Wainwright III as Capt. Calvin Spalding

SYNOPSIS
The 4077 prepares for a visit from Gen. MacArthur.

1. Which surgical procedure does Hawkeye volunteer to perform on Frank?

2. What two things does Klinger promise to not do during MacArthur's visit?

3. What does Margaret put on the bed in the VIP tent?

4. During rehearsals, who stands in for MacArthur?

5. Who or what does Klinger portray on the side of the road as Gen. MacArthur drives through the camp?

EPISODE 3.22 "Payday"

Director: Hy Averback
Written by: John W. Regier and Gary Markowitz

SELECTED SUPPORTING CAST:
Bobbie Mitchell as Lt. Baker
Eldon Quick as Capt. Sloan
Jack Soo as Kim Chung Quoc

SYNOPSIS
Hawkeye is payroll officer and ends up $3,000 richer.

1. What food does Hawkeye hold over steam in the mess tent?

2. How much is the payroll over at first?

3. Who is playing piano in the O Club?

4. What does Hawkeye say Trapper has a gift for?

EPISODE 3.23 "White Gold"

Director: Hy Averback
Written by: Larry Gelbart and Simon Muntner

SELECTED SUPPORTING CAST:
Edward Winter as Col. Samuel Flagg
Hilly Hicks as Cpl. Perkins/Johnson

SYNOPSIS

Col. Flagg appears to investigate an attempted theft of penicillin.

1. How many men infiltrate the 4077 to get to the penicillin?

2. What occupation does Flagg use as his cover?

3. What does Frank do that wakes up Cpl. Perkins?

EPISODE 3.24 "Abyssinia, Henry"

Director: Larry Gelbart
Written by: Everett Greenbaum and Jim Fritzell

SELECTED SUPPORTING CAST:
Gwen Farrell as Nurse Gwen
Kellye Nakahara as Lt. Kellye Yamato

A landmark episode for the show as well as American television, this was also the last episode for both McLean Stevenson and Wayne Rogers.

SYNOPSIS

Henry Blake receives word he is discharged and will be heading back home.

1. What does Radar say happened when he played peek-a-boo the first time with his dad?

2. What does Henry give to Radar?

3. Who is Klinger dressed as when the camp says goodbye to Henry?

4. What does Henry tell Radar he'll do if Radar doesn't behave?

5. Over which sea is Henry's plane shot down over?

SEASON FOUR

STARRING

Alan Alda as Capt. Benjamin Franklin "Hawkeye" Pierce

Mike Farrell as Capt. BJ Hunnicutt

Henry Morgan as Col. Sherman T. Potter

Loretta Swit as Maj. Margaret Houlihan

Larry Linville as Maj. Frank Burns

Gary Burghoff as Cpl. Walter "Radar" O'Reilly

Jamie Farr as Cpl. Max Klinger

William Christopher as Fr. Francis Mulcahy

Trivia answers for Season Four begin on page 291.

EPISODE 4.1 "Welcome to Korea"

Director: Gene Reynolds
Written by: Everett Greenbaum and Jim Fritzell

SYNOPSIS
Hawkeye comes back from R&R to find out Trapper has gone home. When Hawkeye tries to catch him before he leaves, he meets his new cohort, Capt. BJ Hunnicutt.

1. Where does Radar keep his bugle?

2. According to Klinger, which season is it?

3. Who enters camp in a rickshaw?

4. What is Hawkeye wearing as he showers?

5. Who tells Hawkeye Trapper is gone?

6. Who drives the jeep to Kimpo?

7. By how many minutes does Hawkeye miss Trapper?

8. To what imaginary rank does Hawkeye "promote" Radar?

9. What drink does Radar order in the O Club at Kimpo?

10. Where is BJ from?

11. Who drives the jeep back to camp?

12. What article of clothing does BJ lose on his trip to the 4077?

13. Who carries the wounded Korean girl out of the minefield?

14. What does Radar do to the general's car jack before dropping it?

EPISODE 4.2 "Change of Command"

Director: Gene Reynolds
Written by: Jim Fritzell and Everett Greenbaum

SYNOPSIS
Henry's replacement arrives.

1. What does Frank do to protest the change of command?

2. How does Col. Potter announce his arrival to a sunbathing Radar?

3. Who is missing from Col. Potter's meeting with his officers?

4. According to Radar, how long has it been since Potter has performed surgery?

5. Where does Potter say he had a still in WWII?

6. How did Potter get his Purple Heart?

7. What does Potter say his friends call him?

EPISODE 4.3 "It Happened One Night"

Director: Gene Reynolds
Written by: Larry Gelbart and Simon Muntner (teleplay),
    Gene Reynolds (story)

SYNOPSIS
The bitter cold also brings heavy shelling.

1. What does BJ find in the Swamp's coffeepot?

2. What is Hawkeye using for gloves?

3. What is the sentry password?

4. Where does Klinger get "wounded"?

5. How many holes does BJ say are in his patient's colon?

6. What is Klinger's blood type?

7. What explodes in Post Op?

8. In whose tent does Frank fall asleep?

EPISODE 4.4 "The Late Captain Pierce"

Director: Alan Alda
Written by: Glen Charles and Les Charles

SELECTED SUPPORTING CAST
Richard Masur as Lt. "Digger" Detmuller
Eldon Quick as Capt. Pratt

SYNOPSIS
Due to a clerical error, Hawkeye is declared dead.

1. Who wakes BJ when Mr. Pierce calls?

2. Who proposes a wake for Hawkeye?

3. Whose rear end catches fire?

4. What does Hawkeye's blanket get covered in?

5. What gets shoved into Frank's shirt?

6. Which George Orwell book is mentioned by Capt. Pratt?

EPISODE 4.5 "Hey, Doc"

Director: William Jurgensen
Written by: Rick Mittleman

SELECTED SUPPORTING CAST
Frank Marth as Col. Griswald
Bruce Kirby as Sgt. Kimble
Ted Hamilton as Lt. Chivers

SYNOPSIS
A MASH staffer is discharged, but he wants Hawkeye and BJ to help him go by boat rather than by plane.

1. What is Klinger wearing in the shower?

2. According to Hawkeye, what is smarter than Frank?

3. How old was the Scotch whiskey BJ and Hawkeye lost during the sniper attack?

4. Who takes control of the tank?

5. What does Potter do after the tank flattens his jeep?

EPISODE 4.6 "The Bus"

Director: Gene Reynolds
Written by: John D. Hess

SELECTED SUPPORTING CAST
Soon-Tek Oh as Korean Soldier

SYNOPSIS
Radar and the surgeons are stranded and lost when their bus breaks down.

1. Who is driving the bus?

2. How far does Potter instruct his officers to go exploring the area?

3. What kind of plane does Frank see?

4. What food is Frank sneaking?

5. Who does Potter think is more boring asleep than awake?

6. Who takes first watch over the Korean soldier?

7. Who finds Frank's stash of chocolate?

8. Who fixes the bus?

EPISODE 4.7 "Dear Mildred"

Director: Alan Alda
Written by: Everett Greenbaum and Jim Fritzell

SELECTED SUPPORTING CAST
Richard Lee-Sung as Cho

SYNOPSIS
The Potters share another anniversary apart.

1. What does Radar do with the piece of paper he's folding in the first scene?

2. How many years have the Potters been married?

3. Regarding Radar, Potter says the boy is "nice enough, but a little" what?

4. What malady is Mulcahy suffering from?

5. Who does BJ lasso instead of the horse?

6. From what material is Potter's bust carved?

7. Which "language" does Margaret speak to Frank?

8. Where does Radar stash the horse?

EPISODE 4.8 "The Kids"

Director: Alan Alda
Written by: Jim Fritzell and Everett Greenbaum

SELECTED SUPPORTING CAST
Ann Doran as Nurse Meg Cratty
Kellye Nakahara as Lt. Kellye Yamato

SYNOPSIS
Nurse Cratty and the orphans seek shelter at the 4077.

1. What does Hawkeye do when a nurse brings him coffee?

2. How did Frank get his Purple Heart?

3. What does a Korean child call Klinger repeatedly?

4. Who ends up with Frank's medal?

5. What does Radar recover from one of the children?

EPISODE 4.9 "Quo Vadis, Captain Chandler?"

Director: Larry Gelbart
Written by: Burt Prelutsky

SELECTED SUPPORTING CAST
Edward Winter as Col. Samuel Flagg
Allan Arbus as Maj. Sidney Freedman
Alan Fudge as Capt. Arnold Chandler

SYNOPSIS
A wounded man claims to be Jesus Christ.

1. Who does Klinger figure will get his Section 8?

2. According to Margaret and Frank, what are the grounds for a court martial against Capt. Chandler?

3. What superhero does Frank compare Flagg to?

4. Where is Flagg hiding Capt. Chandler's dossier?

5. To what movie monster does Hawkeye compare Flagg?

6. What document did Sidney not sign?

7. What name does Klinger call Flagg?

8. What do we learn is Radar's first name?

9. Who does Klinger impersonate in the last scene?

EPISODE 4.10 "Dear Peggy"

Director: Burt Metcalfe
Written by: Jim Fritzell and Everett Greenbaum

SELECTED SUPPORTING CAST
Ned Beatty as Col. Hollister

Ned Beatty can be recognized from films such as *Deliverance* and *Superman* (1978).

SYNOPSIS
The Divisional Chaplain comes to inspect Father Mulcahy.

1. Which specialty school does BJ say Frank flunked?

2. Who kissed Klinger in his dream?

3. What does Mulcahy affectionately call Hawkeye?

4. What does Frank say is a great way to kill an hour?

5. How many push-ups can Hollister do?

6. What does Klinger inflate in Potter's office?

7. What games is BJ and Hawkeye playing in the last scene?

EPISODE 4.11 "Of Moose and Men"

Director: John Erman
Written by: Jay Folb

SELECTED SUPPORTING CAST
Tim O'Connor as Col. Spiker
Johnny Haymer as Sgt. Zelmo Zale

SYNOPSIS
BJ discovers the slang term of "moose," courtesy of Zale.

1. What is Zale drinking for breakfast?

2. Which of Zale's hands get broken?

3. How much Cherokee blood does Potter say he has?

4. What game is Radar playing over the phone when BJ comes into his office?

5. What does BJ say Radar could have been?

EPISODE 4.12 "Soldier of the Month"

Director: Gene Reynolds
Written by: Linda Bloodworth

SELECTED SUPPORTING CAST
Johnny Haymer as Sgt. Zelmo Zale
Jeff Maxwell as Pvt. Igor Straminsky

SYNOPSIS
Hemorrhagic fever strikes the 4077.

1. Who helps Frank lay out his rat traps?

2. Who writes the answers to the Soldier of the Month quiz on himself?

3. Which two people apply the quiz?

4. How many soldiers take the quiz?

5. Who helps Frank write his will?

6. Which martial art does Radar say he knows?

EPISODE 4.13 "The Gun"

Director: Burt Metcalfe
Written by: Larry Gelbart and Gene Reynolds

SELECTED SUPPORTING CAST
Warren Stevens as Col. Chaffee

SYNOPSIS
A wounded colonel's vintage sidearm goes missing.

1. What is Margaret doing when Radar enters her tent?

2. Which actor does Radar impersonate for Frank?

3. Which two people confront Frank about the missing gun?

4. How many hours does Radar say he sat in a photo booth?

5. What does Frank try to pass off his gunshot wound as to Hawkeye and BJ?

EPISODE 4.14 "Mail Call...Again"

Director: George Tyne
Written by: Jim Fritzell and Everett Greenbaum

SYNOPSIS
Mail from home brings with it surprises for some of the staff.

1. Which actor does Radar imitate?

2. What furnishing does Frank destroy while reading his letter from Louise?

3. How many of his brothers does Klinger say have been killed?

4. Who listens in to Frank's phone conversation with Louise?

5. What does Margaret throw at Frank's head?

6. What is the name of Radar's dog?

EPISODE 4.15 "The Price of Tomato Juice"

Director: Gene Reynolds
Written by: Larry Gelbart and Gene Reynolds

SYNOPSIS
Complications arise when Radar tries to get a regular supply of tomato juice for Col. Potter.

1. What does Klinger ask for from Hawkeye and BJ in return for his help?

2. Who does Potter say Klinger dresses like?

3. Who's using a flyswatter when Radar enters the Swamp?

EPISODE 4.16 "Dear Ma"

Director: Alan Alda
Written by: Everett Greenbaum & Jim Fritzell

SELECTED SUPPORTING CAST
John Fujioka as Col. Kim
Rollin Moriyama as Gen. Park
Byron Chung as Korean Soldier

John Fujioka would also be in episodes "The Tooth Shall Set You Free" (10.14) and "Picture This" (10.20).

SYNOPSIS
Radar's letter home details the goings-on at the camp.

1. Why does Radar tell his mother he's writing slow?

2. Why does Frank have trouble leaving Margaret's tent?

3. What animal is Radar keeping in his office?

4. What is Radar holding for Potter in the OR?

5. Who gives Hawkeye help in examining Frank's feet?

6. What do they find on Frank's toes?

EPISODE 4.17 "Der Tag"

Director: Gene Reynolds
Written by: Everett Greenbaum and Jim Fritzell

SELECTED SUPPORTING CAST
Joe Morton as Capt. Saunders

SYNOPSIS
Col. Potter wants Hawkeye and BJ to treat Frank as a friend.

1. What did Frank once kill with a stick?

2. From who did Mulcahy learn poker?

3. What does Hawkeye say they added to the still for lemon flavor?

4. How much does Frank say he won at poker?

5. What musical instrument does Klinger pretend to play at the O Club?

EPISODE 4.18 "Hawkeye"

Director: Larry Gelbart
Written by: Larry Gelbart and Simon Muntner

SELECTED SUPPORTING CAST
Philip Ahn as The Father
Shizuko Hoshi as The Mother

Philip Ahn is also in "Exorcism" (5.12) and "Change Day" (6.8).

SYNOPSIS
Hawkeye is stranded with a concussion at the home of a Korean family.

1. How many kids are in the family?

2. With what does Hawkeye compare the family's moonshine?

3. What does Hawkeye inflate to amuse the children?

4. Which song from *The King and I* does Hawkeye sing?

5. Which actor does Hawkeye imitate?

EPISODE 4.19 "Some 38th Parallels"

Director: Burt Metcalfe
Written by: John W. Regier and Gary Markowitz

SELECTED SUPPORTING CAST
Kevin Hagen as Col. Coner
Lynette Mettey as Nurse Able
Richard Lee-Sung as Man at Auction

SYNOPSIS
Frank wants to auction off the camp's garbage to the locals.

1. What did Klinger say his dad put in his crib with him?

2. Which song does Hawkeye tell Able he'll be back faster than she can whistle?

3. According to Radar, who confiscated the "best parts" of the Jane Russell jigsaw puzzle?

4. During the auction, what amount does Hawkeye ask BJ to bid over whatever the highest amount is?

5. What act does BJ tell Radar there's no sin in?

6. What game are Hawkeye and Potter playing in the compound?

7. What does Hawkeye have dumped on the departing Col. Coner?

8. In the last scene, what are some of the characters eating popcorn from?

EPISODE 4.20 "The Novocaine Mutiny"

Director: Harry Morgan
Written by: Burt Prelutsky

SELECTED SUPPORTING CAST
Ned Wilson as Col. Carmichael

SYNOPSIS
Frank brings Hawkeye up on charges of mutiny.

1. What did Hawkeye write under Frank's picture of Senator McCarthy?

2. How many service ribbons does Frank wear?

3. What does the group of poker players pretend to be doing when Frank almost catches them playing the game he outlawed?

4. According to Hawkeye's testimony, how did Frank really get knocked out?

EPISODE 4.21 "Smilin' Jack"
Director: Charles Dubin
Written by: Larry Gelbart and Simon Muntner

SELECTED SUPPORTING CAST
Robert Hogan as Lt. Smilin' Jack Mitchell

SYNOPSIS
An affable and ambitious chopper pilot is tested for diabetes.

1. How many soldiers are in the jeep during the mortar attack?

2. What color is Jack's hat?

3. What does Jack do for good luck for the patients he carries?

4. Who nearly gets stabbed with a flying syringe at the O Club?

5. What is the name of the pilot Jack is competing against?

6. What is Hawkeye eating when he, Potter and BJ are in radio contact with Jack?

7. What does Potter answer when asked which was the worst war he'd seen?

EPISODE 4.22 "The More I See You"

Director: Gene Reynolds
Written by: Larry Gelbart and Gene Reynolds

SELECTED SUPPORTING CAST
Blythe Danner as Lt. Carlye Breslin Walton
Mary Jo Catlett as Becky

Blythe Danner has been regularly seen in film, TV and theatre. She is the mother of actress Gwyneth Paltrow.

SYNOPSIS

An old flame that burned Hawkeye is assigned to duty at the camp.

1. What was Klinger doing in the OR when Hawkeye asked Radar about the new nurses?

2. To what does BJ refer to as the 4077 stationery?

3. What does Carlye call the martini Hawkeye serves her in the Swamp?

4. Which animal does Radar impersonate?

5. Why does Mulcahy want to return his shipment of Bibles?

EPISODE 4.23 "Deluge"

Director: William Jurgensen
Written by: Larry Gelbart and Simon Muntner

SYNOPSIS

A downpour doesn't bring anything other than complications.

1. What other war is noted as being fought by the French in a newsreel?

2. What does Radar compare to looking through an ice cube?

3. What does Margaret say made her throw a crying fit when she was five?

4. What animal is shown in a newsreel playing ping-pong?

5. Who puts out the fire outside of OR?

EPISODE 4.24 "The Interview"

Director: Larry Gelbart
Written by: Larry Gelbart

SELECTED SUPPORTING CAST
Clete Roberts as Interviewer

SYNOPSIS
A war correspondent covers the 4077 and its staff.

1. Which book does Hawkeye say he brought over to Korea?

2. What animal does Radar mention as raising?

3. How many amputations does BJ say he performed before his first breakfast in camp?

4. Which personnel does Hawkeye say is not appreciated enough?

5. What does Frank say he misses the most?

SEASON FIVE

STARRING

Alan Alda as Capt. Benjamin Franklin "Hawkeye" Pierce

Mike Farrell as Capt. BJ Hunnicutt

Henry Morgan as Col. Sherman T. Potter

Loretta Swit as Maj. Margaret Houlihan

Larry Linville as Maj. Frank Burns

Gary Burghoff as Cpl. Walter "Radar" O'Reilly

Jamie Farr as Cpl. Max Klinger

William Christopher as Fr. Francis Mulcahy

Trivia answers for Season Five begin on page 299.

EPISODE 5.1 "Bug Out"

Director: Gene Reynolds
Written by: Jim Fritzell and Everett Greenbaum

SELECTED SUPPORTING CAST
Frances Fong as Rosie
Eileen Saki as Korean Woman
James Lough as Enlisted Man

Frances Fong also appears in "Fallen Idol" (6.2).

Eileen Saki would later become Rosie on the show.

James Lough appears in episodes "End Run" (5.17), "Fade Out, Fade In" (6.1), "Commander Pierce" (7.1), "Rally 'Round the Flagg, Boys" (7.21), "Goodbye, Cruel World" (8.21), and "Trick or Treatment" (11.2).

SYNOPSIS
The camp bugs out, but Radar, Hawkeye, and Margaret must stay behind with a patient.

1. How many soldiers are digging the latrine?

2. Why does BJ tell one of the soldiers to dig his side deeper?

3. How many miles away is the camp moving?

4. By what woman's name does a delirious soldier call Frank?

5. How many hours does the camp have to bug out?

6. What does the chopper pilot give Potter to eat?

7. Who tells Hawkeye his wife is looking forward to meeting him?

8. By what mode of transportation does Potter lead the way to the new location?

9. What do the Korean women accept in exchange for the building in the new location?

EPISODE 5.2 "Margaret's Engagement"

Director: Alan Alda
Written by: Gary Markowitz

SYNOPSIS
Margaret returns from Tokyo with surprising news.

1. What does Frank do when he exits the mess tent after hearing of Margaret's engagement?

2. What weapon does Frank accidentally arm?

3. Who takes Frank's rifle from him?

EPISODE 5.3 "Out of Sight, Out of Mind"

Director: Gene Reynolds
Written by: Ken Levine and David Isaacs

SELECTED SUPPORTING CAST
Tom Sullivan as Tom Straw
Enid Kent as Lt. Bigelow
Dudley Knight as Maj. Jim Overman
Judy Farrell as Nurse Able

Actress Judy Farrell was married to Mike Farrell at the time of production.

SYNOPSIS
Hawkeye may be permanently blinded.

1. How many nurses are in the tent when Hawkeye arrives?

2. Which rank does Radar impersonate over the phone?

3. What does Klinger give Hawkeye to signal if he needs help?

4. What is Hawkeye twirling as he speaks to Col. Potter in his office?

EPISODE 5.4 "Lt. Radar O'Reilly"

Director: Alan Rafkin
Written by: Everette Greenbaum and Jim Fritzell

SELECTED SUPPORTING CAST
Johnny Haymer as Sgt. Zelmo Zale
Jeff Maxwell as Pvt. Igor Straminsky

SYNOPSIS
Radar gets a surprise promotion.

1. What does Margaret get in the mail?

2. Which song is Klinger singing while he cuts Potter's hair?

3. To whom does Radar teach the PA system?

EPISODE 5.5 "The Nurses"

Director: Joan Darling
Written by: Linda Bloodworth

SELECTED SUPPORTING CAST
Mary Jo Catlett as Lt. Walsh
Linda Kelsey as Lt. Mickey Baker
Gregory Harrison as Lt. Baker

Gregory Harrison would go on to star in the spinoff that wasn't, *Trapper John, M.D.*

SYNOPSIS
The nurses plot behind Margaret's back.

1. What does BJ put on Mickey when she enters the Swamp?

2. What is Mickey's husband's name?

3. What does Klinger have hanging from his rifle?

EPISODE 5.6 "The Abduction of Margaret Houlihan"

Director: Gene Reynolds
Written by: Allan Katz and Don Reo (teleplay), Gene Reynolds (story)

SELECTED SUPPORTING CAST
Edward Winter as Col. Samuel Flagg

SYNOPSIS
Margaret disappears after late duty.

1. What game is Hawkeye playing when Radar comes into the Swamp?

2. Who does Frank shoot?

3. What did Flagg say he disguised himself as in Las Vegas?

4. What does Radar "give birth" to during the birthing class?

5. How many scorpions does Flagg want Radar to find?

EPISODE 5.7 "Dear Sigmund"

Director: Alan Alda
Written by: Alan Alda

SELECTED SUPPORTING CAST
Allan Arbus as Maj. Sidney Freedman
Sal Viscuso as Patient John
Charles Frank as Capt. Hathaway

Sal Viscuso would appear throughout the series as one of the uncredited voices over the PA as well as act in the episodes "Post Op" (5.23) and "Tea and Empathy" (6.17).
Charles Frank would also be seen on the show in "What's Up, Doc?" (6.19).

SYNOPSIS
Visitor Sidney Freedman writes a letter to Sigmund Freud.

1. What odd footwear is Hawkeye wearing when he does rounds in Post Op?

2. Who does Sidney find reading his letter?

3. What sort of deficiency does Sidney tell Margaret he has?

4. What is Frank digging in the compound?

5. What is Potter standing in while he performs surgery in the last scene?

EPISODE 5.8 "Mulcahy's War"

Director: George Tyne
Written by: Richard Cogan

SELECTED SUPPORTING CAST
Brian Byers as Pvt. Danny Fitzsimmons
Jeff Maxwell as Pvt. Igor Straminsky

SYNOPSIS
Father Mulcahy and Radar go to the front to retrieve a wounded soldier.

1. What is the Military Working Dog's name and rank?

2. Who gives Mulcahy his helmet?

3. What does Mulcahy use to make the incision in the soldier's throat?

4. What does Mulcahy use as a breathing tube?

5. What prayer does Mulcahy say before making the incision?

EPISODE 5.9 "The Korean Surgeon"

Director: Gene Reynolds
Written by: Bill Idelson

SELECTED SUPPORTING CAST
Soon-Tek Oh as Dr. Syn Paik
Robert Ito as North Korean
Larry Hama as North Korean

Larry Hama would go on to write and draw comics, one of which being Marvel's re-launch of the *GI Joe* franchise.

SYNOPSIS
A North Korean surgeon wants to join the 4077.

1. Which surgeon does Paik ask to have operate on him?

2. Who escorts Paik off the evac bus?

3. What rank does Paik become?

4. What did Frank say he sold door-to-door to help get through medical school?

EPISODE 5.10 "Hawkeye Get Your Gun"

Director: William Jurgensen
Written by: Jay Folb (teleplay), Gene Reynolds and Jay Folb (story)

Season Five • 123

SELECTED SUPPORTING CAST
Mako as Major Choi

SYNOPSIS
A South Korean army hospital at the front needs help from Hawkeye and Potter.

1. What does Klinger say he'd rather do than clerk?

2. What is Klinger dressed as when he enters Potter's office while Potter is painting, using Hawkeye as his subject?

3. How do the surgeons determine who goes to the front?

4. What does BJ say he loaded Hawkeye's gun with?

5. Who drives the jeep to the front?

6. What word does Hawkeye say three times that makes him fall asleep?

7. Which poker hand does Klinger draw while he uses cards to see Hawkeye and Potter's fortune?

8. How many shots are fired at Potter and Hawkeye as they flee their jeep?

9. How many shots does Hawkeye fire into the air?

EPISODE 5.11 "The Colonel's Horse"

Director: Burt Metcalfe
Written by: Jim Fritzell and Everett Greenbaum

SELECTED SUPPORTING CAST
Kellye Nakahara as Lt. Kellye Yamato

SYNOPSIS
While Col. Potter is on his second honeymoon, Sophie comes down with colic.

1. What camp contest was Potter entered in?

2. Which legendary swordsman does Hawkeye jokingly refer to himself as?

3. Who nearly gets stabbed by a flying syringe as he enters the Swamp?

4. Who is on top of the water tower?

5. Who walks Margaret around the compound after her surgery?

EPISODE 5.12 "Exorcism"

Director: Alan Alda
Written by: Jay Folb (teleplay), Gene Reynolds and Jay Folb (story)

SELECTED SUPPORTING CAST
Virginia Ann Lee as Kyong Ja
Philip Ahn as Korean Grandfather

SYNOPSIS
A local man refuses to be treated unless an exorcist clears the camp of evil spirits.

1. What do BJ and Hawkeye use to play keep away from Frank?

2. In what day does the episode take place?

3. What does Radar nail to a wall in Potter's office?

4. Who drives the exorcist to the camp?

5. What color is the exorcist's hat?

EPISODE 5.13 "Hawk's Nightmare"

Director: Burt Metcalfe
Written by: Burt Prelutsky

SELECTED SUPPORTING CAST
Allan Arbus as Maj. Sidney Freedman
Patricia Stevens as Lt. Baker

SYNOPSIS
Hawkeye is concerned for his sanity when he begins to sleepwalk and have disturbing nightmares.

1. What does Frank call Margaret when she rebuffs him in Post Op?

2. What is Hawkeye doing during his first sleepwalking episode?

3. How long has it been since Hawkeye has seen his dad?

4. What does Klinger tell Radar will happen to Hawkeye if he wakes up while sleep walking?

EPISODE 5.14 "The Most Unforgettable Characters"

Director: Burt Metcalfe
Written by: Ken Levine and David Isaacs

SELECTED SUPPORTING CAST:
Jeff Maxwell as Pvt. Igor Straminsky

SYNOPSIS
Radar aspires to be a writer.

1. What is the talking animal in the medical school story Hawkeye tells Radar?

2. Whose birthday is it?

3. What does Frank mistake for raisins in his pudding?

4. What position does Mulcahy's sister play on her basketball team?

5. Who tells Frank BJ and Hawkeye aren't mad at each other?

6. Who destroys Frank's watch?

EPISODE 5.15 "38 Across"

Director: Burt Metcalfe
Written by: Jim Fritzell and Everett Greenbaum

SELECTED SUPPORTING CAST
Dick O'Neill as Adm. Cox
Oliver Clark as Lt. Tippy Brooks

Dick O'Neill would also appear in "BJ Papa San" (7.15) and "Sons and Bowlers" (10.19).

Oliver Clark would also star in "Mail Call Three" (6.21).

SYNOPSIS
Hawkeye and BJ need help on a *New York Times* crossword puzzle.

1. Which ship is Tippy on?

2. What is Klinger making a point to eat?

3. What animal does BJ imitate to get the baby to drink the milk?

EPISODE 5.16 "Ping Pong"

Director: William Jurgensen
Written by: Sid Dorfman

SELECTED SUPPORTING CAST
Richard Narita as Cho Lin
Frank Maxwell as Lt. Col. Henry Beckett

SYNOPSIS
The camp's ping-pong champ wants to get married.

1. What color is Cho's hat?

2. For how many days is Cho away?

3. What game are Klinger and Potter playing?

4. Who is the mannequin for the bride's dress?

5. Who cries during the ceremony?

6. What color is Cho's robe?

EPISODE 5.17 "End Run"

Director: Harry Morgan
Written by: John D. Hess

SELECTED SUPPORTING CAST
Henry Brown as Sgt. Billy Tyler
Johnny Haymer as Sgt. Zelmo Zale

SYNOPSIS
A football hero suffers a terrible injury.

1. How many Hawaiian shirts are in the opening bar fight?

2. What food does Klinger throw in Sgt. Zale's face?

3. Who is the ring announcer in the boxing match?

4. Who laughs hysterically when Frank is knocked out?

EPISODE 5.18 "Hanky Panky"

Director: Gene Reynolds
Written by: Gene Reynolds

SELECTED SUPPORTING CAST
Ann Sweeny as Lt. Carrie Donovan

SYNOPSIS

BJ consoles a nurse whose marriage just ended, jeopardizing his own.

1. Who does Margaret accuse of opening her mail?

2. What does BJ say he does at home to get Peg to talk about whatever's bothering her?

3. What is Margaret convinced is Donald's condition?

4. What fictional serial killer does Klinger claim to be?

5. What kind of hernia does Donald have?

EPISODE 5.19 "Hepatitis"

Director: Alan Alda
Written by: Alan Alda

SYNOPSIS

The camp suffers an outbreak of hepatitis.

1. What does Hawkeye throw at BJ in the Swamp?

2. Who draws Frank's blood?

3. What treat does Potter introduce to Hawkeye?

EPISODE 5.20 "The General's Practitioner"

Director: Alan Rafkin
Written by: Burt Prelutsky

SELECTED SUPPORTING CAST
Edward Binns as Gen. Korshack
Leonard Stone as Col. Bidwell
Larry Wilcox as Cpl. Mulligan

Larry Wilcox would go on to star in the hit TV show *CHiPs*.

SYNOPSIS
A general wants Hawkeye to be his personal physician.

1. How many stars does Gen. Korshack have?

2. Who talks to Radar about being a family man?

3. How does Korshack describe Donald?

4. Who wants to be recommended as the general's physician?

5. According to Hawkeye, what did Frank drop in a patient?

EPISODE 5.21 "Movie Tonight"

Director: Burt Metcalfe
Written by: Gene Reynolds, Don Reo, Allan Katz and Jay Folb

SELECTED SUPPORTING CAST
Enid Kent as Lt. Bigelow
Judy Farrell as Lt. Able

SYNOPSIS
Col. Potter's treats the camp to his favorite Western movie.

1. Who does Hawkeye say tried to eat Klinger's mop?

2. What is irregular about the shirt Hawkeye gave to BJ?

3. With what does Margaret threaten Frank?

4. Which movie does Potter have Mulcahy get for the camp?

5. What song does Potter lead the staffers to sing when the film breaks?

6. Who apologizes to Mulcahy before imitating him?

7. During the pretend shootout in the mess tent, who shoots Hawkeye?

Season Five • 133

EPISODE 5.22 "Souvenirs"

Director: Joshua Shelley
Written by: Burt Prelutsky (teleplay), Burt Prelutsky and Reinhold Weege

SELECTED SUPPORTING CAST
Michael Bell as Warrant Officer Stratton
Brian Dennehy as MP Ernie Connors

Writer Reinhold Weege would go on to create TV's *Night Court*.

Both Michael Bell and Brian Dennehy would go on to regular TV and film roles.

SYNOPSIS
The buying and selling of souvenirs causes a problem at the 4077.

1. To what Biblical figure does Hawkeye compare Stratton?

2. Who is getting drunk in the O Club?

3. Who decks Stratton?

4. What name is the 8063rd's CO?

5. How many goldfish did Potter swallow at Camp Grant?

EPISODE 5.23 "Post Op"

Director: Gene Reynolds
Written by: Ken Levine and David Isaacs (teleplay), Gene Reynolds and Jay Folb (story)

SELECTED SUPPORTING CAST
Hilly Hicks as Cpl. Moody
Sal Viscuso as Sgt. Raymond McGill

SYNOPSIS
A blood shortage is the latest calamity for the staff.

1. Who helps a soldier write home?

2. Whose patient has trouble sleeping on his stomach?

3. Who does Hawkeye and BJ have to escort physically to give blood?

EPISODE 5.24 "Margaret's Marriage"

Director: Gene Reynolds
Written by: Everett Greenbaum and Jim Fritzell

SELECTED SUPPORTING CAST
Beeson Carroll as Lt. Col. Donald Penobscott
Patricia Stevens as Lt. Baker
Kellye Nakahara as Lt. Kellye Yamato
Judy Farrell as Lt. Able

Some may recognize Patricia Stevens' voice as Velma from various Scooby-Doo cartoons.

SYNOPSIS
Donald arrives to marry Margaret at the 4077.

1. What song does the staff in the OR sing?

2. Who does Potter foul during a basketball game?

3. What does Klinger give Margaret?

4. Who is passed out in front of the Swamp?

5. Who does a drunk Radar mistake Potter for?

6. According to Hawkeye, how strong is Potter's hangover?

7. Who cries during the wedding?

8. Who catches the bouquet?

9. What does Frank say after Margaret's chopper departs?

SEASON SIX

STARRING

Alan Alda as Capt. Benjamin Franklin "Hawkeye" Pierce

Mike Farrell as Capt. BJ Hunnicutt

Henry Morgan as Col. Sherman T. Potter

Loretta Swit as Maj. Margaret Houlihan

David Ogden Stiers as Maj. Charles Emerson Winchester III

Gary Burghoff as Cpl. Walter "Radar" O'Reilly

Jamie Farr as Cpl. Max Klinger

William Christopher as Fr. Francis Mulcahy

Trivia answers for Season Six begin on page 306.

EPISODE 6.1 "Fade Out, Fade In"

Director: Hy Averback
Written by: Jim Fritzell and Everett Greenbaum

SELECTED SUPPORTING CAST
Robert Symonds as Col. Horace Baldwin

SYNOPSIS
Frank goes berserk while on R&R, and his replacement arrives at the 4077.

1. At what time did Radar say he went to the latrine while waiting for Frank to return to camp?

2. With whom do Hawkeye and BJ have breakfast?

3. What game are Charles and Col. Baldwin playing?

4. How many shells hit around Charles and his driver?

5. How is it explained how Frank got out of the bus he thought Margaret was on?

6. On what does Charles arrive at the camp?

7. What does Margaret find in Frank's effects that Frank said had been stolen by a bellboy?

8. What does Margaret pour into Frank's footlocker?

9. How many MPs escort Schaeffer from Potter's office?

10. What does Hawkeye do to the phone when he's done talking with Frank?

11. What do Hawkeye and BJ put in Charles's bed?

12. Which composer's music is Charles listening to in the Swamp?

EPISODE 6.2 "Fallen Idol"

Director: Alan Alda
Written by: Alan Alda

SELECTED SUPPORTING CAST
Patricia Stevens as Lt. Baker

SYNOPSIS
Radar and his hero Hawkeye have a falling out.

1. How does Radar get wounded?

2. What song does a drunken Hawkeye sing when he enters the Swamp?

3. Who covers for Hawkeye when he has to leave OR?

4. What does Potter say he has a drawer full of?

5. Who is the first person to yell at Hawkeye?

6. Where do Hawkeye and Radar reconcile?

7. What does Hawkeye give Radar at the end of the episode?

EPISODE 6.3 "Last Laugh"

Director: Don Weis
Written by: Everett Greenbaum and Jim Fritzell

SELECTED SUPPORTING CAST
James Cromwell as Leo Bardonaro

James Cromwell's considerable future work in film and TV continues to this date.

SYNOPSIS
An old friend of BJ's causes headaches with his practical jokes.

1. What does Radar sing while he alphabetizes?

2. What animal is Klinger pretending to bring into Potter's office?

3. What article of clothing proves BJ is innocent?

EPISODE 6.4 "War of Nerves"

Director: Alan Alda
Written by: Alan Alda

SELECTED SUPPORTING CAST
Allan Arbus as Maj. Sidney Freedman
Michael O'Keefe as Tom
Johnny Haymer as Sgt. Zelmo Zale
Peter Riegert as Cpl. Igor Straminsky

Michael O'Keefe was in a similar role in the episode "Mad Dogs and Servicemen."

It may be worth noting Jeff Maxwell is not in the role of Igor Straminsky. The character has a new/temporary rank of corporal.

SYNOPSIS
The 4077 has a bonfire to relieve tensions.

1. From which army are the uniforms that are burned?

2. Who is the first to visit Sidney?

3. What concern does Klinger bring to Sidney?

4. What classic TV comedy is mentioned by Sidney?

5. What does Klinger throw onto the bonfire?

6. What do BJ and Hawkeye throw into the fire?

EPISODE 6.5 "The Winchester Tapes"

Director: Burt Metcalfe
Written by: Everett Greenbaum and Jim Fritzell

SYNOPSIS
Charles sends a tape-recording home asking for help in leaving Korea.

1. Of whom is Potter painting a portrait?

2. What does Radar use to clean Potter's paint brushes?

3. What does BJ give to Charles to help him gain weight?

4. What is BJ pretending to dust when Charles enters the Swamp?

5. What does Charles find in his teapot?

EPISODE 6.6 "The Light That Failed"

Director: Charles Dubin
Written by: Burt Prelutsky

SYNOPSIS
A mystery novel arrives at the 4077, along with other frustrating things.

1. What horror film legend does Hawkeye imitate?

2. What rank is the delivery truck driver?

3. What is the name of the mystery novel?

4. What is the author's name?

5. Who calls Margaret "Jessica"?

6. What drug does Charles accidently give a patient?

7. According to Hawkeye, why can't Charles work in the dark?

EPISODE 6.7 "In Love and War"

Director: Alan Alda
Written by: Alan Alda

SELECTED SUPPORTING CAST
Kieu Chinh as Kyung Soon
Enid Kent as Lt. Bigelow
Susan Krebs as Lt. Gleason

SYNOPSIS
A once well-to-do Korean civilian turns Hawkeye's head.

1. What does Hawkeye diagnose Kyung's mother as having?

2. How far away is Kyung's water supply?

3. What language does Kyung ask Hawkeye if he speaks?

4. How does Hawkeye describe a hawk?

EPISODE 6.8 "Change Day"

Director: Don Weis
Written by: Laurence Marks

SELECTED SUPPORTING CAST
Phillip Ahn as Mr. Kim
Tom Dever as Cpl. Boone

Tom Devers would appear in the episodes "Deal Me Out," "Aid Station," "Welcome to Korea," and "They Call the Winter Korea."

SYNOPSIS
Charles comes up with a way to make a profit on a new military scrip.

1. From what color to what color is the scrip changing to?

2. How much does Charles pay for the old scrip?

3. In which language does Charles say goodbye to the Korean civilians?

4. Which branch of the service does Klinger claim to be a part of when Charles returns to camp?

EPISODE 6.9 "Images"

Director: Burt Metcalfe
Written by: Burt Prelutsky

SELECTED SUPPORTING CAST
Susan Blanchard as Lt. Cooper

Prior to *MASH*, Susan Blanchard would be familiar as Marie Endicott Martin on the long-running soap opera *All My Children*.

SYNOPSIS
Margaret sees one of her nurses as a liability.

1. Which classic painter has Radar never heard of?

2. What does Radar order at Rosie's?

3. What "tattoo" does Radar get?

EPISODE 6.10 "The M*A*S*H Olympics"

Director: Don Weis
Written by: Ken Levine and David Isaacs

SELECTED SUPPORTING CAST
Mike Henry as Lt. Col. Donald Penobscott
Michael McManus as Sgt. Ames

SYNOPSIS
Potter has the camp participate in 4077-style Olympic events.

1. How many MPs turn the ambulance back on its tires?

2. How many countries are noted as participating in the 1952 Helsinki Olympics?

3. In what is the unit's Olympic flame burning?

4. What is the name of Hawkeye's team?

5. What is the name of BJ's team?

6. What was the score tied at?

7. What is the last event?

EPISODE 6.11 "The Grim Reaper"

Director: George Tyne
Written by: Burt Prelutsky

SELECTED SUPPORTING CAST
Charles Aidman Col. Victor Bloodworth

SYNOPSIS
A visiting colonel brings Hawkeye up on charges of assault.

1. Who takes over for Charles when he gets sick in surgery?

2. What does Hawkeye call Col. Bloodworth's ledger?

3. What is wrong with the pilot's jacket?

4. Who ends up with the jacket?

5. Which doctor operates on Col. Bloodworth?

EPISODE 6.12 "Comrades in Arms. Part One"

Director: Burt Metcalfe and Alan Alda
Written by: Alan Alda

SELECTED SUPPORTING CAST
Johnny Yune as North Korean

Actor Johnny Yune also appeared in the episodes "Exorcism" and "The Abduction of Margaret Houlihan."

SYNOPSIS
Margaret and Hawkeye find solace in each other's arms.

1. How many cans of cling peaches does Potter give them to see if they can be bargained for penicillin?

2. What is the 8063's motto?

3. What does Hawkeye do to try to fix the jeep?

4. How many enemy soldiers take the jeep?

5. What is Klinger dressed in when Charles enters Potter's office?

6. In which leg does Hawkeye get wounded in?

EPISODE 6.13 "Comrades in Arms. Part 2"

Director: Alan Alda and Burt Metcalfe
Written by: Alan Alda

SELECTED SUPPORTING CAST
Doug Rowe as Aylesworth

SYNOPSIS
Margaret and Hawkeye return to camp from their harrowing trip.

1. What do Hawkeye and Margaret have for breakfast?

2. Who meets BJ and Aylesworth when they return to the helipad?

3. Who carries Margaret into the mess tent?

4. What the first gift given to Hawkeye and Margaret?

5. Who gives them the gift?

6. What name does Margaret use to address her letter to Donald?

EPISODE 6.14 "The Merchant of Korea"

Director: William Jurgensen
Written by: Ken Levine

SELECTED SUPPORTING CAST
Johnny Haymer as Sgt. Zelmo Zale

SYNOPSIS
Hawkeye and BJ both end up owing Charles money, and the major won't let them forget it.

1. What's the first favor Charles asks of BJ?

2. What does Hawkeye do to help the nurses stay cool?

3. What's the tab maximum at the O Club?

EPISODE 6.15 "The Smell of Music"

Director: Stuart Millar
Written by: Jim Fritzell and Everett Greenbaum

SELECTED SUPPORTING CAST
Jordan Clarke as Pvt. Saunders

SYNOPSIS
Hawkeye and BJ stop showering in protest to Charles's musicianship.

1. What instrument does Charles play?

2. What does Hawkeye use as a mute in Charles's horn?

3. What does Margaret call Charles's French horn?

EPISODE 6.16 "Patent 4077"

Director: Harry Morgan
Written by: Ken Levine and David Isaacs

SELECTED SUPPORTING CAST
Keye Luke as Mr. Shin
Johnny Haymer as Sgt. Zelmo Zale

Keye Luke is also in the episodes "A Night at Rosie's" and "Death Takes a Holiday" and may be best known to audiences as Master Po of TV's *Kung Fu*.

SYNOPSIS
The doctors need to invent a new surgical instrument.

1. What is inscribed on Margaret's ring?

2. Who watches BJ and Hawkeye try to modify a clamp?

3. Who refers to himself as a master craftsman?

4. Which part of Klinger's body gets burned looking for Margaret's ring?

5. Whose hand gets stuck in the new clamp?

6. How much does Mr. Shin charge to make the new clamp?

EPISODE 6.17 "Tea and Empathy"

Director: Don Weis
Written by: Bill Idelson

SELECTED SUPPORTING CAST
Bernard Fox as Major Ross
Sal Viscuso as Cpl. Benny Bryant

Character actor Bernard Fox would be familiar for his very British roles throughout his career.

SYNOPSIS
Father Mulcahy must use the black market to get much-needed penicillin.

1. What does Hawkeye say is an old American saying?

2. From which country is the Gloucester Regiment?

3. What color is the hat Klinger wears to the schoolhouse?

4. Which article of clothing does Klinger rip/lose?

EPISODE 6.18 "Your Hit Parade"

Director: George Tyne
Written by: Ronny Graham

SELECTED SUPPORTING CAST
Ronny Graham as Sgt. Gribble
Johnny Haymer as Sgt. Zelmo Zale

Writer/actor Ronny Graham would work on future episodes as story consultant.

SYNOPSIS
Radar plays DJ to the camp during a high influx of casualties for the morale of the staff.

1. What game have BJ and Hawkeye come up with?

2. Who volunteers the use of Charles's phonograph?

3. Who coaches Radar on how to use DJ lingo?

4. Which song does Potter keep requesting?

5. With whom do Hawkeye and BJ temporarily bunk with?

6. What's the advice Sgt. Gribble gives about the Swamp's gin?

EPISODE 6.19 "What's Up, Doc?"

Director: George Tyne
Written by: Larry Balmagia

SELECTED SUPPORTING CAST
Charles Frank as Lt. Martinson

SYNOPSIS
A patient holds Charles prisoner.

1. What fictional detective does Hawkeye imitate in OR?

2. What is the name of Radar's rabbit?

3. Which Ivy League college did Lt. Martinson attend?

EPISODE 6.20 "Mail Call Three"

Director: Charles Dubin
Written by: Everett Greenbaum and Jim Fritzell

SELECTED SUPPORTING CAST
Oliver Clark as Capt. Ben Pierce

SYNOPSIS
Hawkeye's mail gets switched with another Capt. Ben Pierce.

1. What article does Charles find in the store room?

2. Who is annoyed at the chatter during the movie?

3. Which two characters sing together in the O Club?

4. Who wakes Radar to use the phone?

5. In the last scene, who passes out in the O Club?

EPISODE 6.21 "Temporary Duty"

Director: Burt Metcalfe
Written by: Larry Balmagia

SELECTED SUPPORTING CAST
George Lindsey as Capt. Roy Dupree
Marcia Rodd as Capt. Lorraine Anderson
Enid Kent as Lt. Bigelow

George Lindsey may be best known for his character of Goober on *The Andy Griffith Show*.

SYNOPSIS
The 4077 and 8063 temporarily swap a surgeon and a nurse.

1. What collective nickname did Margaret and Lorraine share?

2. Whose name does Dupree get wrong almost during his entire stay?

3. Which two articles of civilian clothing does Dupree wear?

4. What game are Charles and BJ playing when Hawkeye returns to the Swamp?

EPISODE 6.22 "Potter's Retirement"

Director: William Jurgensen
Written by: Laurence Marks

SELECTED SUPPORTING CAST
George Wyner as Cpl. Benson

SYNOPSIS
Someone in the camp is sending negative reports about Potter's command to I Corps.

1. How long does Potter have until retirement?

2. What does BJ use for the mint in the mint juleps?

3. Who pretends to be an MP?

4. Who calls Potter by his first name?

EPISODE 6.23 "Dr. Winchester and Mr. Hyde"

Director: Charles Dubin
Written by: Ken Levine, David Isaacs and Ronny Graham

SELECTED SUPPORTING CAST
Chris Murney as Remy
Joe Tornatore as Sgt. Solita

SYNOPSIS
Charles resorts to the use of amphetamines to get through the grueling schedule.

1. What classic novel is referenced in Post Op?

2. What is the name of the Marines' mouse?

3. What is the name of Radar's mouse?

4. Where does Charles keep the bottle of amphetamines?

EPISODE 6.24 "Major Topper"

Director: Charles Dubin
Written by: Allyn Freeman

SELECTED SUPPORTING CAST
Hamilton Camp as Cpl. "Boots" Miller
Kellye Nakahara as Lt. Kellye Yamato

Hamilton Camp would also be in episodes "The Moon Is Not Blue" (11.8) and the series finale, "Goodbye, Farewell, and Amen."

SYNOPSIS
The 4077 deals with a batch of bad morphine.

1. Which singer does Boots imitate?

2. Who insists the placebos won't work?

3. Who helps Hawkeye and BJ make the placebos?

4. How many shots does Boots fire at the enemy glider?

5. How many gliders does Boots claim to have shot down?

6. Which actress has Charles dated?

SEASON SEVEN

STARRING

Alan Alda as Capt. Benjamin Franklin "Hawkeye" Pierce

Mike Farrell as Capt. BJ Hunnicutt

Henry Morgan as Col. Sherman T. Potter

Loretta Swit as Maj. Margaret Houlihan

David Ogden Stiers as Maj. Charles Emerson Winchester III

Gary Burghoff as Cpl. Walter "Radar" O'Reilly

Jamie Farr as Cpl. Max Klinger

William Christopher as Fr. Francis Mulcahy

Trivia answers for Season Seven begin on page 312.

EPISODE 7.1 "Commander Pierce"

Director: Burt Metcalfe
Written by: Ronny Graham (teleplay), Ronny Graham and Don Segall (story)

SELECTED SUPPORTING CAST
James Lough as Webster
Andrew Masset as Hough

SYNOPSIS
Hawkeye takes temporary command.

1. What is Potter doing in his sleep?

2. What does Hawkeye say is his insignia?

3. What color is the towel Charles is using to trap steam?

4. What does Klinger give Potter in the last scene?

EPISODE 7.2 "Peace on Us"

Director: George Tyne
Written by: Ken Levine and David Isaacs

SELECTED SUPPORTING CAST
Hugh Gillin as Gen. Tomlin
Kevin Hagen as Maj. Dean Goss

Kevin Hagen also played Col. Coner in "Some 38th Parallels."

SYNOPSIS
Hawkeye crashes the peace talks.

1. What kind of table does Hawkeye say the delegates should negotiate over?

2. How does Margaret exit the office after her phone call?

3. How many MPs are at the checkpoint?

4. What medical condition does Tomlin have?

5. What has BJ on his surgical mask?

EPISODE 7.3 "Lil"

Director: Burt Metcalfe
Written by: Sheldon Bull

SELECTED SUPPORTING CAST
Carmen Mathews as Col. Lillian Rayburn

SYNOPSIS
A head nurse from Potter's generation visits the 4077.

1. How long does Lil say she's been in the Army?

2. What does Potter bring to Lil's tent?

3. Who does Margaret have a drink with in the O Club?

4. Which song are Potter and Lil singing as they enter the camp?

EPISODE 7.4 "Our Finest Hour Part One and Part Two"

Director: Burt Metcalfe
Written by: Ken Levine, David Isaacs, Larry Balmagia, Ronny Graham and David Lawrence

SELECTED SUPPORTING CAST
Clete Roberts as Himself

SYNOPSIS
Clete Roberts returns to the 4077. Past shows are seen in retrospect.

1. Who is the first character Roberts speaks with?

2. What does Radar say he misses the most?

3. What does BJ miss?

4. Who has trouble saying something nice about Charles?

EPISODE 7.5 "The Billfold Syndrome"

Director: Alan Alda
Written by: Ken Levine and David Isaacs

SELECTED SUPPORTING CAST
Kevin Geer as Sgt. Jerry Nielson

SYNOPSIS
A medic the staff knows becomes an amnesiac.

1. What is Klinger doing at the start of the episode?

2. Which part of the human body does Pierce compare to a tank?

3. What does BJ call Radar's filing?

EPISODE 7.6 "None Like It Hot"

Director: Tony Mordente
Written by: Ken Levine, David Isaacs and Johnny Bonaduce

SELECTED SUPPORTING CAST
Johnny Haymer as Sgt. Zelmo Zale
Jeff Maxwell as Pvt. Igor Straminsky
Kellye Nakahara as Lt. Kellye Yamato
Ted Gehring as Sgt. Rhoden

Jeff Maxwell returns as Igor, as does the character's original rank.

SYNOPSIS
Hawkeye and BJ's bathtub arrives during a sweltering heat wave.

1. What is BJ using to fan himself in the opening scene?

2. From where do Hawkeye and BJ get the tub?

3. Who is the first to use the tub?

4. What do Potter and Radar use to mitigate Klinger's stench?

5. What does Hawkeye tell Radar he blindfolded to ensure Radar's privacy in the tub?

6. How does Hawkeye respond when Sgt. Rhoden asks if he's a Commie?

7. Which flavor ice cream does Radar want?

EPISODE 7.7 "They Call the Wind Korea"

Director: Charles Dubin
Written by: Ken Levine and David Isaacs

SELECTED SUPPORTING CAST
Enid Kent as Lt. Bigelow
Tom Dever as MP

SYNOPSIS
Charles and Klinger get lost in a windstorm.

1. What is Potter sitting on in the opening scene?

2. What color are BJ's suspenders?

3. Which lullaby does Radar sing to his guinea pig?

4. Which nurse gets injured when the water tower falls?

5. From which country are the wounded soldiers in the truck?

6. How old did Charles say he was when he dissected his first frog?

7. What does Margaret give Bigelow in Post Op?

8. What novelty item is Hawkeye wearing when he visits the little boy in Post Op?

EPISODE 7.8 "Major Ego"

Director: Alan Alda
Written by: Larry Balmagia

SELECTED SUPPORTING CAST
Greg Mullavey as Capt. Tom Greenleigh

SYNOPSIS
A reporter from *Stars and Stripes* arrives to interview Charles.

1. What drink does Mulcahy serve in OR?

2. Who poses for a picture with Charles?

3. What color is Klinger's Scarlett O'Hara dress?

4. Who is tending bar when Margaret is in the O Club?

5. Which *Wizard of Oz* character does Klinger dress as?

EPISODE 7.9 "Baby, It's Cold Outside"

Director: George Tyne
Written by: Gary David Goldberg

SELECTED SUPPORTING CAST
Jan Jorden as Lt. Baker

SYNOPSIS
The 4077 treats troops with hypothermia.

1. Which animal do Hawkeye and BJ imitate?

2. What color is Charles's polar suit?

3. What article of clothing does Charles give to Margaret?

4. Where does BJ threaten to hide Radar's glasses?

5. What effect does chocolate have on Radar?

6. What did the police in Toledo call Klinger?

EPISODE 7.10 "Point of View"

Director: Charles Dubin
Written by: Ken Levine and David Isaacs

SELECTED SUPPORTING CAST
Hank Ross as Ferguson
David Stafford as Pvt. Rich

SYNOPSIS
We see a wounded soldier's time at MASH 4077 through his eyes.

1. Including Rich, how many men are in Rich's squad?

2. Where is Pvt. Rich wounded?

3. Which two people take Rich off the chopper?

4. What does Margaret do that makes Pvt. Rich grab her hand?

EPISODE 7.11 "Dear Comrade"

Director: Charles Dubin
Written by: Tom Reeder

SELECTED SUPPORTING CAST
Sab Shimono as Kwang

Sab Shimono would appear in "Back Pay" (8.24).

SYNOPSIS
The man Charles has hired as a houseboy is a North Korean spy.

1. What is Charles doing in the first scene?

2. What gift did BJ and Hawkeye get for Charles while in Tokyo?

3. How does Kwang describe Charles in his letter to his comrades?

4. Where does Hawkeye throw the howitzer's firing pin?

5. What do Hawkeye and BJ pour down the howitzer's barrel?

EPISODE 7.12 "Out of Gas"

Director: Mel Damski
Written by: Tom Reeder

SELECTED SUPPORTING CAST
Johnny Haymer as Sgt. Zelmo Zale
Byron Chung as Myung

SYNOPSIS
Father Mulcahy must use his black market connections to get a supply of sodium pentothal.

1. What game is being played in the opening scene?

2. To which unit did Zale trade the 4077's shipment of sodium pentothal?

3. Which two characters go to the black marketeers?

4. How many black marketeers are there?

5. In what vehicle do Mulcahy and Charles use to escape the black marketeers?

EPISODE 7.13 "An Eye for a Tooth"

Director: Charles Dubin
Written by: Ronny Graham

SELECTED SUPPORTING CAST
Peter Palmer as Capt. Toby Hill

SYNOPSIS
A series of pranks masterminded by Charles escalate to a dangerous level.

1. What is Potter doing in his office when Mulcahy comes to see him?

2. What kind of pie does Klinger deliver to Margaret?

3. Who ends up getting hit with the pie?

EPISODE 7.14 "Dear Sis"

Director: Alan Alda
Written by: Alan Alda

SELECTED SUPPORTING CAST
Jeff Maxwell as Pvt. Igor Straminsky
Jo Ann Thompson as Nurse Jo Ann

SYNOPSIS
Father Mulcahy writes a letter to his sister.

1. In which holiday season does the episode take place?

2. What does Potter say are growing on the back of his tongue?

3. What animal does Radar want Mulcahy to say a blessing for?

4. Who talks Mrs. O'Reilly through the delivery of the calf?

5. Who tends bar at the O Club when Margaret and Klinger are there?

6. What was Potter's gift to Radar?

7. Who portrays Santa Claus?

EPISODE 7.15 "BJ Papa-San"

Director: James Sheldon
Written by: Larry Balmagia

SELECTED SUPPORTING CAST
Johnny Haymer as Sgt. Zelmo Zale
Mariel Aragon as Kim Sing
Dick O'Neill as Brigadier General Marion Prescott
Shizuko Hoshi as Mother
Chao Li Chi as Father

Chao Li Chi would also appear in "As Time Goes By" (11.15).

SYNOPSIS
A Korean family comes to rely on BJ's help.

1. Where is Gen. Prescott first injured?

2. What's the name of Radar's queen bee?

3. Which part of the family's house does BJ repair?

4. What's the name of the bee that stings Gen. Prescott?

5. What Cole Porter song is Hawkeye singing in OR during the shelling?

6. What happens to Gen. Prescott's jeep as he is leaving camp?

EPISODE 7.16 "Inga"

Director: Alan Alda
Written by: Alan Alda

SELECTED SUPPORTING CAST
Mariette Hartley as Dr. Inga Halvorsen

Mariette Hartley's considerable work in acting continues to this writing.

SYNOPSIS
A visiting Swedish doctor makes Hawkeye rethink his approach to women.

1. Which composer's music does Hawkeye put on when Inga visits the Swamp?

2. Which part of Inga's anatomy does Hawkeye compliment?

3. On what article of BJ's clothing does Hawkeye demonstrate heart surgery?

4. With what does Margaret tell Hawkeye she could replace his lips?

EPISODE 7.17 "The Price"

Director: Charles Dubin
Written by: Erik Tarloff

SELECTED SUPPORTING CAST
Yuki Shimoda as Cho Pak
Miko Mayama as Sun

Other episodes with Yuki Shimoda are "Yessir, That's Our Baby" (8.15) and "Oh, How We Danced" (9.14).

SYNOPSIS
Potter's horse, Sophie, goes missing.

1. By which mode of transportation does Potter enter camp?

2. To what color does Potter say his underpants have turned?

3. Who insists they left the stable door open?

4. What do Hawkeye and BJ have Ham wear as a disguise?

5. Where does Ham hide from the Republic of Korea?

EPISODE 7.18 "The Young and the Restless"

Director: William Jurgensen
Written by: Mitch Markowitz

SELECTED SUPPORTING CAST
James Canning as Capt. Ralph Simmons

SYNOPSIS
A young doctor has a profound effect on Potter and Charles.

1. Who does Potter wake up in the opening scene?

2. Who interrupts the surgeons' meeting?

3. Who enters the Swamp drunk?

4. What does a hungover Charles wear on his head in the mess tent?

5. What question does Potter ask of Klinger to trip his latest attempt at a Section 8?

EPISODE 7.19 "Hot Lips is Back in Town"

Director: Charles Dubin
Written by: Larry Balmagia and Bernard Dilbert (teleplay),
    Bernard Dilbert and Gary Markowitz (story)

SELECTED SUPPORTING CAST
Peggy Lee Brennan as Lt. Linda Nugent
Walter Brooke as Gen. Lyle Weiskopf

SYNOPSIS
Margaret's mood after her divorce motivates her to come up with a new way to handle triage.

1. What is Potter's grandson's name?

2. What song is Mulcahy playing on the piano in the O Club?

3. Which two staffers are drinking with Margaret at the O Club?

4. Which rank does Gen. Weiskopf offer to Margaret?

5. To whom does Margaret propose a toast to after Gen. Weiskopf leaves her tent?

EPISODE 7.20 "C*A*V*E"

Director: William Jurgensen
Written by: Larry Balmagia and Ronny Graham

SELECTED SUPPORTING CAST
Basil Hoffman as Maj. Bartruff
Mark Taylor as O'Malley

SYNOPSIS
The 4077 must relocate to a cave during intense shelling.

1. Where is Klinger hiding during the shelling?

2. What is Potter's answer to Maj. Bartruff's authentication phrase?

3. Who is riding in the jeep with Klinger on the way to the cave?

4. What does Hawkeye insist will happen if he enters the cave?

5. What does Hawkeye yell when he runs back into the cave?

6. Which two characters share the same blood type as Klinger?

7. Which historical figure is Margaret thinking of during the game of 20 Questions with Hawkeye?

EPISODE 7.21 "Rally 'Round the Flagg, Boys"

Director: Harry Morgan
Written by: Mitch Markowitz

SELECTED SUPPORTING CAST
Edward Winter as Col. Samuel Flagg
James Carroll as MP
Jerry Fujikawa as Hung Pak
Bob Okazaki as Doo Pak

Bob Okazaki would appear in "The Yalu Brick Road" (8.10).

SYNOPSIS
Col. Flagg investigates Hawkeye as a Communist sympathizer.

1. Which card game is being played in the opening scene?

2. With what body part does Flagg threaten Charles with?

3. In what does Flagg hide during his first meeting with Charles?

4. Who stops Flagg when he threatens the North Korean's IV?

5. Who fools Flagg, thwarting his investigation?

EPISODE 7.22 "Preventative Medicine"

Director: Tony Mordente
Written by: Tom Reeder

SELECTED SUPPORTING CAST
James Wainwright as Col. Lacy

SYNOPSIS
Hawkeye finds himself on questionable ethical ground as a doctor.

1. Which US state does BJ say the X-ray of a wounded man's liver looks like?

2. What does Col. Lacy try to give his men in Post Op?

3. What does Hawkeye use as a mortar pestle when Lacy is in the Swamp?

4. Which organ does Hawkeye remove from Col. Lacy?

EPISODE 7.23 "A Night at Rosie's"

Director: Burt Metcalfe
Written by: Ken Levine and David Isaacs

SELECTED SUPPORTING CAST
Eileen Saki as Rosie
Kellye Nakahara as Lt. Kellye Yamato

Joshua Bryant as Sgt. Jerry Scully

SYNOPSIS
The staff have an extended stay at Rosie's.

1. How long does Hawkeye tell Rosie he's been in surgery?

2. Who first comes looking for Hawkeye and BJ?

3. What is Hawkeye doing when Charles comes to Rosie's?

4. Who is Officer of the Day?

5. In the craps game, who sees the dice get switched?

6. Who is Margaret dancing with when the MPs enter Rosie's?

7. Who tries to stop the barfight?

8. Who gets hit by a piece of flying wood during the barfight?

9. What does BJ have stuck in his hair after the fight?

EPISODE 7.24 "Ain't Love Grand?"

Director: Mike Farrell
Written by: Ken Levine and David Isaacs

SELECTED SUPPORTING CAST
Sylvia Chang as Sooni
Kit McDonough as Lt. Debbie Clark

SYNOPSIS
Klinger falls hard for a visiting nurse.

1. To which composer's music is Charles listening to in the opening scene?

2. To which MASH unit is Lt. Clark attached?

3. Which class of uniform is Klinger wearing while serving in the mess tent?

4. What game is Mulcahy hosting at the O Club?

5. Where does Hawkeye sleep rather than the Swamp?

6. How does BJ celebrate the good news about his kidney patient?

7. Which song does Charles sing with Klinger at the O Club?

EPISODE 7.25 "The Party"

Director: Burt Metcalfe
Written by: Alan Alda and Burt Metcalfe

SELECTED SUPPORTING CAST
Kellye Nakahara as Lt. Kellye Yamato
Burt Metcalfe as Driver

SYNOPSIS
BJ has an idea for a party in the States for the families of the 4077 staff during a bug out.

1. In which tent does the first scene take place in?

2. How long does Margaret say her parents have been separated?

3. Who drives Potter back to the 4077?

4. According to Radar on the return trip, which part of the truck "won't stay on the road"?

5. Who tells BJ the party is on?

6. Which sport does Mulcahy's sister play?

7. Who doesn't want the picture of the MASH personnel taken at the camp's signpost?

SEASON EIGHT

STARRING

Alan Alda as Capt. Benjamin Franklin "Hawkeye" Pierce

Mike Farrell as Capt. BJ Hunnicutt

Henry Morgan as Col. Sherman T. Potter

Loretta Swit as Maj. Margaret Houlihan

David Ogden Stiers as Maj. Charles Emerson Winchester III

Gary Burghoff as Cpl. Walter "Radar" O'Reilly

Jamie Farr as Cpl. Max Klinger

William Christopher as Fr. Francis Mulcahy

Trivia answers for Season Eight begin on page 320.

EPISODE 8.1 "Too Many Cooks"

Director: Charles S. Dubin
Written by: Dennis Koenig

SELECTED SUPPORTING CAST
John Randolph as Gen. Budd Haggerty
Ed Begley, Jr. as Pvt. Paul Conway

Ed Begley, Jr. would go on to a considerable amount of TV and film work.

SYNOPSIS
Col. Potter's marriage is strained.

1. How did Conway get wounded?

2. What color is Klinger's nightcap?

3. What impressive, improvised meal does Conway make?

4. Which brand of shoes are hanging from the Swamp's stovepipe?

5. What is being used as a table for BJ, Hawkeye, Potter, Mulcahy and Margaret when they are in Klinger's mess tent restaurant?

6. From where was Mildred writing Potter from?

EPISODE 8.2 "Are You Now, Margaret?"

Director: Charles S. Dubin
Written by: Thad Mumford and Dan Wilcox

SELECTED SUPPORTING CAST
Lawrence Pressman as Congressional Aide R. Theodore Williamson

SYNOPSIS
Margaret is investigated on grounds of sedition.

1. With what is BJ entertaining himself when Hawkeye and Williamson enter the Swamp?

2. According to BJ, what did Charles used to be?

3. What make of car does Margaret say an ex-boyfriend had?

EPISODE 8.3 "Guerilla My Dreams"

Director: Alan Alda
Written by: Bob Colleary

SELECTED SUPPORTING CAST
Mako as Lt. Hung Lee Park
Haunani Minn as Guerilla Woman

It may be of interest to learn that this episode marks the first time the phrase "son of a bitch" aired on an American television network.

SYNOPSIS
The surgeons try to save a female POW suspected as being a guerilla who does not want to be saved.

1. Which doctor is in charge of the prisoner?

2. Who does Klinger call for help?

3. Who distracts the South Korean soldiers?

4. What does Klinger say the Army gave his nose?

5. Who tries to block Lt. Park from exiting the O Club?

EPISODE 8.4 "Good-Bye, Radar: Part 1"

Director: Charles S. Dubin
Written by: Ken Levine and David Isaacs

SELECTED SUPPORTING CAST
Michael O'Dwyer as Olsen
Marilyn Jones as Lt. Patty Haven

SYNOPSIS
Radar's Uncle Ed has passed away and Radar will be going home.

1. Who does Klinger argue with at the generator?

2. How much of a bribe does Radar offer Olsen?

3. How many soldiers get into Radar's jeep?

EPISODE 8.5 "Good-Bye, Radar: Part 2"

Director: Charles S. Dubin
Written by: Kem Levine and David Isaacs

SELECTED SUPPORTING CAST
Michael O'Dwyer as Olsen
Marilyn Jones as Lt. Patty Haven

SYNOPSIS
Radar contemplates staying at the 4077.

1. What does Margaret do to Radar when he enters Post Op?

2. Radar tells Potter without him the camp will be "up a tree without" what?

3. What rhetorical question does Klinger ask when Hondo calls?

4. Who is the only one to call Radar "Walter" when saying goodbye to him?

5. What does the driver say about Radar's hometown?

6. Where does Radar leave his teddy bear?

7. Who finds Radar's teddy bear?

EPISODE 8.6 "Period of Adjustment"

Director: Charles S. Dubin
Written by: Jim Mulligan and John Rappaport

SELECTED SUPPORTING CAST
Whitney Rydbeck as Hondo

SYNOPSIS
Radar may be gone, but his presence is still felt at the camp, especially for BJ and Klinger.

1. According to Potter, how many weeks have passed since Radar's departure?

2. What does Klinger tell Margaret he lost?

3. While in the mess tent, what does Klinger ask Igor to give him a slice of?

4. Who warns Hawkeye about BJ's marked drunkenness?

5. Which animal does Potter say Klinger couldn't find in a foot locker?

6. How does BJ gain access to Potter's liquor cabinet?

7. What does Hawkeye put on before going to Potter's office to retrieve BJ?

EPISODE 8.7 "Nurse Doctor"

Director: Charles S. Dubin
Written by: Sy Rosen, Thad Mumford and Dan Wilcox (teleplay), Sy Rosen (story)

SELECTED SUPPORTING CAST
Alexandra Stoddart as Lt. Gail Harris
Kellye Nakahara as Lt. Kellye Yamato

SYNOPSIS
Father Mulcahy is the object of affection of one of the nurses.

1. In the first scene, how many seconds of shower-time does Potter tell Hawkeye he has left?

2. Which surgeon's technique does Lt. Harris question?

3. What's Fr. Mulcahy's first name?

EPISODE 8.8 "Private Finance"

Director: Charles S. Dubin
Written by: Dennis Koenig

SELECTED SUPPORTING CAST
Mark Kologi as Pvt. Eddie Hastings
Art Evans as Dolan
Shizuko Hoshi as Mrs. Li

Shizuko Hoshi would also appear in "BJ Papa-San," "Hawkeye," and "Mad Dogs and Servicemen."

SYNOPSIS
A mortally wounded soldier entrusts Hawkeye to send a huge sum of money to his parents.

1. With what does Mrs. Li try to hit Klinger?

2. With what does Mrs. Li try to *stab* Klinger?

3. What does Klinger use to keep the pitchfork at bay?

4. Who goes with Potter to talk to Mrs. Li?

EPISODE 8.9 "Mr. and Mrs. Who?"

Director: Burt Metcalfe
Written by: Ronny Graham

SELECTED SUPPORTING CAST
Claudette Nevins as Donna Marie Parker

SYNOPSIS
Charles returns from R&R… newly married.

1. Who returns to camp hung over?

2. Which book of the Bible is Shaw reading?

3. By what percentage of salt does Hawkeye suggest for the IVs?

4. By which name does Donna refer to Charles?

5. Who performs the unwedding ceremony?

6. What does BJ read from while performing the unwedding?

EPISODE 8.10 "The Yalu Brick Road"

Director: Charles S. Dubin
Written by: Mike Farrell

SELECTED SUPPORTING CAST
Soon-Teck Oh as Ralph

SYNOPSIS
Hawkeye and BJ are stuck behind enemy lines.

1. What caused the outbreak of salmonella?

2. Who is driving the jeep when it crashes?

3. What name does Hawkeye give the Chinese soldier?

4. What does Hawkeye name the farmer?

5. Who carries Fred back to his farm?

EPISODE 8.11 "Life Time"

Director: Alan Alda
Written by: Alan Alda and Walter D. Dishell, M.D.

SELECTED SUPPORTING CAST
Kevin Brophy as Roberts
Kellye Nakahara as Lt. Kellye Yamato
Joann Thompson as Nurse Jo Ann

SYNOPSIS
The clock is ticking in (more-or-less) real time on a patient with a lacerated aorta.

1. What game is being played when the chopper lands?

2. Who has the winning hand?

3. Who brings the ice into the OR?

4. Who has to rummage through Hawkeye's footlocker to find the clamps he needs?

5. Whose hand is frozen from the ice?

6. Who does Klinger impersonate to get information about incoming casualties?

7. Who has the same blood type as the wounded soldier?

8. What does Charles say to the nurse prepping him for the transfusion?

EPISODE 8.12 "Dear Uncle Abdul"

Director: William Jurgensen
Written by: John Rappaport and Jim Mulligan

SELECTED SUPPORTING CAST
Richard Lineback as Eddie
Alexander Petale as Cpl. Hank Fleming

SYNOPSIS
A letter home from Klinger detailing the goings-on at the 4077.

1. Who proposes the Korean War needs a song?

2. What is Potter painting?

3. Where does Hawkeye tell the joke about the circus?

4. Who composes the song for the Korean War?

5. Who takes care of Eddie until he gets wounded?

6. Who takes over watching Eddie for Hank?

EPISODE 8.13 "Captains Outrageous"

Director: Burt Metcalfe
Written by: Thad Mumford and Dan Wilcox

SELECTED SUPPORTING CAST
G.W. Bailey as The G.I.
John Orchard as MP Muldoon
Sirri Murad as The Turk
Eileen Saki as Rosie

John Orchard previously played "Ugly" John in the series. G.W. Bailey would become a familiar face at MASH as Sgt. Luther Rizzo.

SYNOPSIS
The surgeons help manage Rosie's.

1. Who gets hurt in the fight at Rosie's?

2. Who proposes the MASH surgeons cover for Rosie?

3. What does Rosie use to calculate profit?

4. What does Potter refer to as a "monument to Murphy's Law"?

5. Who gives Mulcahy his captain's bars?

EPISODE 8.14 "Stars and Stripes"

Director: Harry Morgan
Written by: Dennis Koenig

SELECTED SUPPORTING CAST
Joshua Bryant as Pvt. Jack Scully
Jeff Maxwell as Pvt. Igor Straminsky

SYNOPSIS
BJ and Charles butt heads as they try to write a medical article together.

1. What does Charles share with BJ to celebrate their article?

2. What did Scully do to get demoted?

3. What does Scully's CO call him?

4. Who is the first person with whom Hawkeye plays Scrabble?

5. Who helps Margaret alter her dress?

6. In the last scene, with whom does Hawkeye play Scrabble?

EPISODE 8.15 "Yessir, That's Our Baby"

Director: Alan Alda
Written by: Jim Mulligan

SELECTED SUPPORTING CAST
Howard Platt as Maj. Ted Spector
Yuki Shimoda as Chung Ho Kim
William Bogert as Roger Prescott

William Bogert would appear in "Depressing News" (9.12)

SYNOPSIS
An infant of American father and Korean mother is left on the Swamp's doorstep.

1. Who finds the baby?

2. Who helps Charles read the note left with the baby?

3. Which two people go to the Red Cross?

4. Who demonstrates the diapering process?

EPISODE 8.16 "Bottle Fatigue"

Director: Burt Metcalfe
Written by: Thad Mumford and Dan Wilcox

SELECTED SUPPORTING CAST
Shelley Long as Lt. Mendenhall

Shelley Long would find fame as Diane Chambers on *Cheers*.

SYNOPSIS
Hawkeye's sobering bar tab prompts a trip on the wagon.

1. What does Charles call the "grape Nehi of alcoholic beverages"?

2. What does Charles order in the opening scene in the O Club?

3. Who helps Charles with his phone call to the States?

4. What does Hawkeye call a drunken Charles?

EPISODE 8.17 "Heal Thyself"

Director: Mike Farrell
Written by: Dennis Koenig (teleplay), Dennis Koenig and Gene Reynolds (story)

SELECTED SUPPORTING CAST
Edward Herrmann as Capt. Steven J. Newsome

SYNOPSIS
With Potter and Winchester down with mumps, a replacement surgeon is called in from Tokyo.

1. Who wins the "volleyball" match when Newsome enters the Swamp?

2. Where was Newsome originally stationed?

3. Which card game are Charles and Potter playing?

4. How does Charles refer to Zane Grey?

5. Which opera singer is Charles listening to?

6. In whose tent does Newsome end up?

7. Who joins Potter and Charles in quarantine in the last scene?

EPISODE 8.18 "Old Soldiers"

Director: Charles S. Dubin
Written by: Dennis Koenig

SYNOPSIS
The staff cares for a group of orphans and worries about their CO.

1. Which fairy tale is Klinger telling a Korean girl?

2. According to Potter, which animal is "a noble beast"?

3. What does Potter share with the young Korean boy?

EPISODE 8.19 "Morale Victory"

Director: Charles S. Dubin
Written by: John Rappaport

SELECTED SUPPORTING CAST
James Stephens as Pvt. David Sheridan

SYNOPSIS
Charles helps a soldier suffering from a hand crippled in combat.

1. Hawkeye refers to sitting through the same movie being shown once again as "A recurring nightmare with..." what?

2. What does Hawkeye and BJ want Klinger to build for them?

3. What is the civilian occupation of Pvt. Sheridan?

4. What does Mulcahy insist on having before addressing the crow in the mess tent?

5. What is BJ doing in the Swamp when he and Hawkeye talk about the beach picnic?

6. What is inside Klinger's footlocker when he delivers the crabs?

EPISODE 8.20 "Lend a Hand"

Director: Alan Alda
Written by: Alan Alda

SELECTED SUPPORTING CAST
Robert Alda as Dr. Anthony Borelli
Antony Alda as Cpl. Jarvis

The late Antony Alda was the brother of Alan.

SYNOPSIS
Dr. Borelli returns to the 4077, much to the consternation of Hawkeye.

1. What is Hawkeye's favorite color?

2. According to Borelli, what causes hangovers in Scotch and soda?

3. Who was in charge of decorating the cake?

4. Who is the first to volunteer for the trip to Battalion Aid?

5. What is Hawkeye eating on the trip to the aid station?

EPISODE 8.21 "Goodbye, Cruel World"

Director: Charles S. Dubin
Written by: Thad Mumford and Dan Wilcox

SELECTED SUPPORTING CAST
Allan Arbus as Maj. Sidney Freedman
Clyde Kusatsu as Sgt. Michael Yee

SYNOPSIS
Hawkeye calls Sidney to help with a suicidal patient.

1. What does Klinger do to his office?

2. What does Potter call Klinger's decorations?

3. Whose signature does Klinger practice?

4. What does Sidney use to hypnotize Yee?

5. What is the one item of Klinger's that Potter allows to be put up in the office?

6. According to Kellye, how long was Sgt. Yee under hypnosis?

EPISODE 8.22 "Dreams"

Director: Alan Alda
Written by: Alan Alda (teleplay), Alan Alda and James Jay Rubinfier (story)

SELECTED SUPPORTING CAST
Fred Stuthman as Professor
Catherine Bergstrom as Peg Hunnicutt

SYNOPSIS
The staff suffers nightmares during a seemingly never-ending glut of wounded.

1. What is Margaret dressed in during her dream?

2. Who does BJ dream of?

3. What enters Potter's office during his dream?

4. What does Charles do in his dream?

5. How does Mulcahy see himself in his dream?

6. Where does Klinger dream he is?

7. Who wakes up Klinger?

8. Who is sitting with Hawkeye at the start of his dream?

EPISODE 8.23 "War Co-Respondent"

Director: Mike Farrell
Written by: Mike Farrell

SELECTED SUPPORTING CAST
Susan Saint James as Aggie O'Shea

Susan Saint James was well-known to TV audiences prior to her appearance on *MASH*, as a cast member of *The Name of the Game* and *McMillan & Wife*.

SYNOPSIS
Hawkeye tries desperately to impress a visiting war correspondent.

1. What does Hawkeye ask Aggie for?

2. What does BJ ask for?

3. In what subject does Aggie school BJ?

EPISODE 8.24 "Back Pay"

Director: Burt Metcalfe
Written by: Thad Mumford, Dan Wilcox and Dennis Koenig

SELECTED SUPPORTING CAST
Richard Herd as Capt. Bill Snyder
G.W. Bailey as Sgt. Luther Rizzo
Sab Shimono as Jin
Jerry Fujikawa as Wu
Peter Kim as Po

SYNOPSIS
Hawkeye decides to bill the Army for his work.

1. Who sends Hawkeye the newspaper clipping that upsets him?

2. Who brings the bag of X-rays to Hawkeye?

3. What comedians do Charles call the Korean doctors?

4. Who tries to help Charles's back with moist heat?

EPISODE 8.25 "April Fools"

Director: Charles S. Dubin
Written by: Dennis Koenig

SELECTED SUPPORTING CAST
Pat Hingle as Col. Daniel Webster Tucker
G.W. Bailey as Sgt. Luther Rizzo

SYNOPSIS
April Fool's Day at the camp, just in time for an uptight colonel's visit.

1. What animal does Hawkeye say he was hungry enough to eat?

2. What is in the can of pralines BJ gives to Charles?

3. Who puts the minnows in Margaret's pocket?

4. What do the surgeons put on Potter's coattail?

5. What is Col. Tucker's favorite drink?

6. Potter calls BJ, Margaret, and Hawkeye a "Pack of…" what?

SEASON NINE

STARRING

Alan Alda as Capt. Benjamin Franklin "Hawkeye" Pierce

Mike Farrell as Capt. BJ Hunnicutt

Henry Morgan as Col. Sherman T. Potter

Loretta Swit as Maj. Margaret Houlihan

David Ogden Stiers as Maj. Charles Emerson Winchester III

Jamie Farr as Cpl. Max Klinger

William Christopher as Fr. Francis Mulcahy

Trivia answers for Season Nine begin on page 327.

EPISODE 9.1 "The Best of Enemies"

Director: Charles S. Dubin
Written by: Sheldon Bull

SELECTED SUPPORTING CAST
Mako as Lin Han

SYNOPSIS
A North Korean soldier captures Hawkeye.

1. What is the main color of Hawkeye's civilian shirt?

2. What does BJ throw at a singing Hawkeye?

3. Who is the first Charles asks to team with him?

4. Who acts as commentator during the bridge game?

EPISODE 9.2 "Letters"

Director: Charles S. Dubin
Written by: Dennis Koenig

SELECTED SUPPORTING CAST
Richard Paul as Capt. Bill Bainbridge
Eileen Saki as Rosie
Michael Currie as Dr. Breuer

SYNOPSIS
The personnel respond to letters from Hawkeye's hometown.

1. What is the name of the dog Mulcahy cures of drinking alcohol?

2. Which animal is Klinger breeding?

3. What does Mulcahy's letter writer say they'd rather be doing than writing a letter?

4. What is Potter doing while answering his letter?

EPISODE 9.3 "Cementing Relationships"

Director: Charles S. Dubin
Written by: David Pollock and Elias Davis

SELECTED SUPPORTING CAST
Joel Brooks as Corpsman Ignazio De Simone

SYNOPSIS
The 4077 installs a concrete floor in OR.

1. From which country is Margaret's unwanted love interest from?

2. Who refuses to work on the floor?

3. Who is made the foreman of the project?

4. Who makes the caution signs?

EPISODE 9.4 "Father's Day"

Director: Alan Alda
Written by: Karen L. Hall

SELECTED SUPPORTING CAST
Andrew Duggan as Col. Alvin "Howitzer" Houlihan

SYNOPSIS
Margaret's father visits the 4077.

1. Who tells Potter his hair could use a trim?

2. What does Margaret do before she hugs her father?

3. What is the marking on Hawkeye's crate?

4. Which part of the OR could Col. Houlihan not handle?

EPISODE 9.5 "Death Takes a Holiday"

Director: Mike Farrell
Written by: Mike Farrell, John Rappaport and Dennis Koenig (teleplay), Thad Mumford, Dan Wilcox and Burt Metcalfe (story)

SELECTED SUPPORTING CAST
Keye Luke as Choi Sung Ho
Kellye Nakahara as Lt. Kellye Yamato

SYNOPSIS
Christmas at MASH 4077 finds the camp hosting orphans and a single casualty.

1. What is in BJ's package from home?

2. To where does Charles deliver the chocolates?

3. How does Kellye describe macadamia nuts to the kids?

EPISODE 9.6 "A War for All Seasons"

Director: Burt Metcalfe
Written by: Dan Wilcox and Thad Mumford

SELECTED SUPPORTING CAST
Roy Goldman as Snapshooting Corpsman
Kellye Nakahara as Lt. Kelley Yamato
Jeff Maxwell as Pvt. Igor Straminsky

SYNOPSIS
An entire year at MASH 4077 in a single episode.

1. In which season does the episode begin?

2. At the New Year's party, who portrays the old year of 1950?

3. From where did Hawkeye and BJ get their coats?

4. Which section of the catalogue does Mulcahy want to see?

5. Which song are BJ and Hawkeye listening to on their new radio?

6. Where does Potter's fly ball land?

7. How many games were the Dodgers up by on July 4th?

8. What does Igor do to the corn, much to Mulcahy's displeasure?

9. What does Charles spit into while listening to the game over the PA?

10. Which team's cap does Charles wear?

11. Where does Klinger hide from Charles?

12. Which team wins the pennant?

EPISODE 9.7 "Your Retention, Please"

Director: Charles S. Dubin
Written by: Erik Tarloff

SELECTED SUPPORTING CAST
Barry Corbin as Sgt. Joe Vickers

SYNOPSIS
A retention officer comes to the 4077.

1. Who declines Vickers in the O Club?

2. Who accepts Vickers's re-enlistment pitch?

3. Which oath does Potter have Klinger pledge?

4. Who is Klinger portraying as he rides Sophie?

EPISODE 9.8 "Tell It to the Marines"

Director: Harry Morgan
Written by: Hank Bradford

SELECTED SUPPORTING CAST
Michael McGuire as Col. Mulholland
Stan Wells as Jost Van Liter

SYNOPSIS
Hawkeye and BJ try to help an immigrant serving in the US Marines.

1. In the opening scene, for how long does Hawkeye say he's going to sleep?

2. From which country is Van Liter?

3. Which song is Klinger whistling in his office?

4. With which flower does Charles have Klinger garnish his breakfast?

5. Where is the press train located?

6. How does Potter refer to the music Charles is listening to?

EPISODE 9.9 "Taking the Fifth"

Director: Charles S. Dubin
Written by: Elias Davis and David Pollock

SELECTED SUPPORTING CAST
Judy Farrell as Lt. Able
Jan Jorden as Lt. Baker

SYNOPSIS
Hawkeye obtains a bottle of vintage wine and looks for a nurse to share it with.

1. Where does the opening scene take place in?

2. Which drug do the doctors want to use for their patients but are not allowed?

3. How much money does Klinger owe Hawkeye?

4. What is the nickname of the nurse Hawkeye picks to share his wine?

5. Which part of the jeep Klinger and Potter ride in causes a problem?

EPISODE 9.10 "Operation Friendship"

Director: Rena Down
Written by: Dennis Koenig

SELECTED SUPPORTING CAST
Tim O'Connor as Capt. Norman Traeger

O'Connor also appeared in "Of Moose and Men."

SYNOPSIS
Klinger saves Charles's life in an accident that leaves BJ seriously injured.

1. Who gets blown into a wall by the explosion?

2. What part of Klinger's body get broken?

3. What part of BJ's body is injured?

4. Which book does Klinger have Charles read to him?

EPISODE 9.11 "No Sweat"

Director: Burt Metcalfe
Written by: John Rappaport

SYNOPSIS
An evening at the 4077 during a heat wave.

1. What piece of equipment has Klinger taken apart?

2. What line of work does Klinger tell Potter he wants to get into after the war?

3. Why does Potter go into his office in the middle of the night?

4. Who wakes up Margaret?

5. What does a sleeping pill-addled Potter try to use as a phone?

6. What is Charles working on in the mess tent?

7. What does Charles go looking for in Klinger's office?

8. Who turns the fan on in the mess tent?

9. Where are Hawkeye and BJ when Klinger accidentally broadcasts Potter and Margaret's conversation?

EPISODE 9.12 "Depressing News"

Director: Alan Alda
Written by: Dan Wilcox and Thad Mumford

SELECTED SUPPORTING CAST
William Bogert as Capt. Maurice Allen

SYNOPSIS
Hawkeye creates a monument to the wounded.

1. What is the name of Klinger's camp newspaper?

2. How many years' worth of tongue depressors does BJ say the camp now has?

3. Who writes the names of the wounded on the tongue depressors?

EPISODE 9.13 "No Laughing Matter"

Director: Burt Metcalfe
Written by: Elias Davis and David Pollock

SELECTED SUPPORTING CAST
Robert Symonds as Col. Horace Baldwin

SYNOPSIS
The colonel responsible for sending Charles to the 4077 comes to the camp.

1. Which magazine do Potter, Hawkeye, and BJ discuss in the O Club?

2. Which seafood does Charles ask Potter if he's had?

3. What game do Charles and Col. Baldwin play?

EPISODE 9.14 "Oh, How We Danced"

Director: Burt Metcalfe
Written by: John Rappaport

SELECTED SUPPORTING CAST
Catherine Bergstrom as Peg Hunnicutt
Yuki Shimoda as Key Yong Lu
Arlen Dean Snyder as Maj. Finch

SYNOPSIS
Hawkeye engineers a surprise for the anniversary BJ must spend away from Peg.

1. What is Charles dictating into his tape recorder in the Swamp when BJ and Hawkeye enter?

2. What does Charles will to his sister?

3. According to BJ, how far along was Peg in her pregnancy on their last anniversary?

4. Who interviews BJ about his life back home?

5. Who does Hawkeye impersonate in his phone call to Maj. Finch?

6. What piece of furniture does Charles break during his showdown with Finch?

7. Who dances with BJ?

EPISODE 9.15 "Bottoms Up"

Director: Alan Alda
Written by: Dennis Koenig

SELECTED SUPPORTING CAST
Gail Strickland as Capt. Helen Whitfield

SYNOPSIS
A friend of Margaret's struggles with alcoholism.

1. What card game is Helen and Margaret playing in the opening scene?

2. Which blood type does Margaret ask Helen for in OR?

3. In what place is Charles when he sits in the glue?

4. What is Potter doing in his office when Klinger tells him about finding Helen in the storeroom?

5. Where does BJ find himself after Hawkeye and Charles move him in his sleep?

EPISODE 9.16 "The Red/White Blues"

Director: Gabrielle Beaumont
Written by: Elias Davis and David Pollock

SELECTED SUPPORTING CAST
Kellye Nakahara as Lt. Kellye Yamato
Jo Ann Thompson as Nurse Jo Ann

SYNOPSIS
The staff try to help Potter's blood pressure from going through the roof.

1. Who gives Potter his physical?

2. Where does Klinger want to go for R&R?

3. Why does Potter lose his temper with Klinger?

4. According to Potter, who is the only one who isn't killing him with kindness?

5. Who does Margaret put in charge of stalling Potter from going into his office?

EPISODE 9.17 "Bless You, Hawkeye"

Director: Nell Cox
Written by: Dan Wilcox and Thad Mumford

SELECTED SUPPORTING CAST
Allan Arbus as Maj. Sidney Freedman

SYNOPSIS
With a severe case of sneezing and itching, Hawkeye fears he's dying.

1. In his office, what does Potter give to Mulcahy to pass to Hawkeye?

2. Where is Hawkeye quarantined?

3. Who does Potter call to help Hawkeye?

4. Where does the last scene take place?

EPISODE 9.18 "Blood Brothers"

Director: Harry Morgan
Written by: David Pollock and Elias Davis

SELECTED SUPPORTING CAST
G.W. Bailey as Sgt. Luther Rizzo
Ray Middleton as Cardinal Reardon
Patrick Swayze as Pvt. Gary Sturgis

Viewers will of course recognize Patrick Swayze from his later work in *Dirty Dancing* and *Road House*.

SYNOPSIS
An upcoming visit from his superior has Father Mulcahy on edge.

1. What day is the cardinal to arrive?

2. Who berates some of the staff for playing craps?

3. What is the name of the illustrated pin-up girl in the O Club?

4. Who breaks the news to Sturgis that he has leukemia?

5. Who arrives late for the Sunday service?

EPISODE 9.19 "The Foresight Saga"

Director: Charles S. Dubin
Written by: Dennis Koenig

SELECTED SUPPORTING CAST
Philip Sterling as Dr. Myron "Bud" Herzog
Rummel Mor as Park Sung

SYNOPSIS
The 4077 hears that Radar's farm is struggling.

1. Who "wakes" a BJ feigning sleep in the opening scene?

2. How does Radar refer to himself at the end of his letter?

3. What does Dr. Herzog say Margaret may need one of these days?

4. Who treats Park Sung's wounds?

5. According to Potter, who broke his watch?

6. Who talks to Mrs. O'Reilly on the phone?

EPISODE 9.20 "The Life You Save"

Director: Alan Alda
Written by: John Rappaport and Alan Alda

SELECTED SUPPORTING CAST
Val Bisoglio as The Cook
Andrew Parks as Dying Soldier
G.W. Bailey as Sgt. Luther Rizzo

SYNOPSIS
Charles nearly gets killed and develops a fascination with death.

1. In which location in the 4077 does the opening scene take place?

2. What piece of medical equipment gets shattered by a sniper's bullet?

3. In what article of his uniform does Charles find the bullet hole?

4. Who questions Charles's change in behavior?

5. Who identifies himself as "the idiot" who stuck Hawkeye with the missing trays?

6. What is the dying soldier's reply when Charles asks him "What is happening to you?"

SEASON TEN

STARRING

Alan Alda as Capt. Benjamin Franklin "Hawkeye" Pierce

Mike Farrell as Capt. BJ Hunnicutt

Henry Morgan as Col. Sherman T. Potter

Loretta Swit as Maj. Margaret Houlihan

David Ogden Stiers as Maj. Charles Emerson Winchester III

Jamie Farr as Cpl. Max Klinger

William Christopher as Fr. Francis Mulcahy

Trivia answers for Season Ten begin on page 333.

EPISODE 10.1 "That's Show Biz"

Director: Charles S. Dubin
Written by: David Pollock and Elias Davis

SELECTED SUPPORTING CAST
Gwen Verdon as Brandy Doyle
Danny Dayton as Fast Freddie Nichols
Gail Edwards as Marina Ryan
Karen Landry as Sarah Miller
Amanda McBroom as Ellie Carlyle

As viewers may guess by her performance, Amanda McBroom is a musician of high caliber, having composed several hit songs, including Bette Midler's "The Rose."

SYNOPSIS
A USO troupe makes an emergency detour to the 4077.

1. What does a soldier give to Margaret on the chopper pad?

2. Who identifies Brandy as a stripper?

3. What musical instrument does Sarah hold as she's greeting the MASH staff?

4. Which doctor finds Fast Freddie's jokes funny?

5. What color is Brandy's feather boa?

6. What unique kind of shoes are Sarah looking for from her brother's effects?

7. Who dances with Kellye in the O Club?

8. Who starts to write jokes during the USO's visit?

9. Which classic comedian does Mulcahy sarcastically refer to Klinger as?

EPISODE 10.2 "Identity Crisis"

Director: David Ogden Stiers
Written by: Dan Wilcox and Thad Mumford

SELECTED SUPPORTING CAST
Dirk Blocker as James Mathes
Joe Pantoliano as Cpl. Gerald Mullen/Josh Levin
Shari Saba as Nurse Shari

Joe Pantoliano would become a popular actor known for work such as *The Matrix* and *Memento*.

SYNOPSIS
A wounded soldier is posing as a deceased friend to get discharged.

1. Who is the first person to invest in Security Fidelity?

2. In which language does Mulcahy say he's a little rusty?

3. Whose picture does Klinger give to Hawkeye?

EPISODE 10.3 "Rumor at the Top"

Director: Charles S. Dubin
Written by: David Pollock and Elias Davis

SELECTED SUPPORTING CAST
Nicholas Pryor as Maj. Nathaniel Burnham

SYNOPSIS
The staff fears a rumor that they will be broken up when the Army wants a new MASH unit.

1. How many times has Gen. Torgeson been married?

2. Who warns Klinger about starting any rumors?

3. Who spreads the rumor to BJ?

4. Which city's archdiocese is "honoring" Father Mulcahy?

5. What "god" does Klinger invoke to Maj. Burnham?

EPISODE 10.4 "Give 'Em Hell, Hawkeye"

Director: Charles S. Dubin
Written by: Dennis Koenig

SELECTED SUPPORTING CAST
Stefan Gierasch as Col. Ditka
Lance Toyoshima as Kim Han
Kellye Nakahara as Lt. Kellye Yamato

SYNOPSIS
Hawkeye pays a visit to the peace talks.

1. What does Hawkeye say is the only thing the peace delegates can agree on?

2. Who takes the role of foreman in the beautification of the compound?

3. Which of the doctors does Kim Han approach for his operation?

4. Whose talk with Kim Han changes his mind?

EPISODE 10.5 "Wheelers and Dealers"

Director: Charles S. Dubin
Written by: Thad Mumford and Dan Wilcox

SELECTED SUPPORTING CAST
G.W. Bailey as Sgt. Luther Rizzo

SYNOPSIS
Following a citation for reckless driving, Col. Potter must take a driving test.

1. What arrives in Klinger's office in the opening scene?

2. In which Korean city is Potter cited for reckless driving?

3. Who is the MASH driving instructor?

4. Which poker hand does Hawkeye see BJ has failed to make?

5. What color is the kimono Margaret wears during the poker game?

6. Who talks to Hawkeye about BJ's erratic behavior?

7. What game is BJ playing when Hawkeye and Margaret confront him at the O Club?

EPISODE 10.6 "Communication Breakdown"

Director: Alan Alda
Written by: Karen Hall

SELECTED SUPPORTING CAST
Byron Chung as Lt. Yook
James Saito as Park

SYNOPSIS
With nothing to read for weeks, Charles gets a shipment of newspapers from home.

1. Which comic strip does Col. Potter follow?

2. Who discovers Charles's newspapers?

3. Which issue of *The Boston Globe* is missing?

4. What must Charles cover himself with when his clothes are stolen from the showers?

5. What item of Charles's gets taken from the Swamp?

6. Who admits they saw who took it?

7. In whose tent are Charles's pilfered effects stored in?

8. Who informs Charles about the wildcat trucker's strike that caused the missing newspaper to not be delivered?

EPISODE 10.7 "Snap Judgement"

Director: Hy Averback
Written by: Paul Perlove

SELECTED SUPPORTING CAST
Peter Jurasik as Capt. Triplett

Science Fiction fandom would recognize Peter Jurasik's later work in TV's *Babylon 5*.

SYNOPSIS
Hawkeye's Polaroid camera is stolen.

1. Which drug is being stolen from the camp?

2. Which baseball team's jersey is Klinger wearing?

3. What did Klinger send to I Corps instead of the stolen goods report?

4. Who tells Klinger about Little Chicago?

5. Who takes a self-portrait with the Polaroid?

EPISODE 10.8 "Snappier Judgement"

Director: Hy Averback
Written by: Paul Perlove

SELECTED SUPPORTING CAST
Peter Hobbs as Col. Drake

SYNOPSIS
The investigation into Hawkeye's camera continues.

1. Who represents Klinger in court?

2. Who erupts in gales of laughter while trying to read the script Charles has prepared?

3. Who uses Charles's tape recorder as bait for the real thief?

4. In court, who is the first witness?

5. Charles uses a Latin phrase in court he is told to translate. What is the translation?

EPISODE 10.9 "'Twas the Day After Christmas"

Director: Burt Metcalfe
Written by: Elias Davis and David Pollock

SELECTED SUPPORTING CAST
Val Bisoglio as Sgt. Pernelli
Michael Ensign as Major Cass

SYNOPSIS
The staff of the 4077 change places on Boxing Day.

1. Which Christmas song is Mulcahy singing?

2. Who educates Klinger on what Boxing Day is?

3. Who trades responsibilities with Klinger?

4. According to Klinger, how many "damns" a minute is Potter typing?

5. Which weather condition is headed for the 4077?

6. Who informs Potter his morale is at an all-time low?

7. What does Kellye say is all she wants?

EPISODE 10.10 "Follies of the Living—Concerns of the Dead"

Director: Alan Alda
Written by: Alan Alda

SELECTED SUPPORTING CAST
Kario Salem as Pvt. Jimmy Weston

SYNOPSIS
A soldier dies at the 4077, his spirit wandering the camp, and only a feverish Klinger can see him.

1. What medical condition does Potter say Klinger is suffering from?

2. Which relative does a hallucinating Klinger think Charles is?

3. What is Klinger carrying as he stumbles across the compound?

4. Which eating utensil does Margaret tell BJ he's picky about?

5. What is the name of the soldier Weston sees in OR?

6. What kind of condition are BJ, Charles, and Hawkeye in when Weston visits them in the Swamp?

EPISODE 10.11 "The Birthday Girls"

Director: Charles S. Dubin
Written by: Karen Hall

SELECTED SUPPORTING CAST
Jerry Fujikawa as Lee Tsung

SYNOPSIS
Margaret wants to spend her birthday in Tokyo.

1. Who is waiting in Klinger's office for a phone call?

2. Who does Margaret ask to stand in for her at the nurses' lecture?

3. Which game is BJ and Hawkeye playing in the Swamp?

4. At the lecture, who asks Charles to go slower so the nurses can take notes?

5. Who offers to make Margaret a birthday hat out of newspaper?

6. What sort of hats does Margaret say she hates?

7. What does Potter call his fist?

8. What does Klinger use as a candle in the muffin he gives to Margaret?

9. Who wins the calf lottery?

EPISODE 10.12 "Blood and Guts"

Director: Charles S. Dubin
Written by: Lee H. Grant

SELECTED SUPPORTING CAST
Gene Evans as Clayton Kibbee
Rita Wilson as Nurse Lacey

Rita Wilson was also in "Hey, Look Me Over" (11.1), and later went on to films such as *Sleepless in Seattle* and *Runaway Bride* and would marry Tom Hanks.

SYNOPSIS
A war correspondent is not above sensationalizing the war for his readers.

1. Who is driving the jeep Kibbee arrives in?

2. Which surgeon is a motorcycle enthusiast?

3. What make and model is the motorcycle BJ inherits?

4. Who confronts Kibbee about the fiction he puts in his stories?

5. What color is BJ's motorcycle?

EPISODE 10.13 "A Holy Mess"

Director: Burt Metcalfe
Written by: David Pollock and Elias Davis

SELECTED SUPPORTING CAST
Cyril O'Reilly as Pvt. Nick Gillis
David Graf as Lt. Spears

SYNOPSIS
A distraught soldier seeks sanctuary from Father Mulcahy.

1. Who is the first character to speak in the episode?

2. How does Pooter want his eggs?

3. Who disarms Pvt. Gillis?

4. Where does Charles sarcastically say Klinger keeps his cheese?

5. What theme for the brunch does BJ and Hawkeye announce?

EPISODE 10.14 "The Tooth Will Set You Free"

Director: Charles S. Dubin
Written by: David Pollock and Elias Davis

SELECTED SUPPORTING CAST
Tom Atkins as Maj. Lawrence Weems
Jason Bernard as Capt. Quentin Rockingham
Larry Fishburne as Cpl. Dorsey
John Fujioka as Duc Phon Jong

Audiences may know Larry Fishburne as he became better known. Laurence Fishburne.

SYNOPSIS
A racist major needs to be dealt with.

1. What type of Army personnel have been wounded?

2. Hawkeye says a patient has been shot how many times?

3. What are Mulcahy and Dorsey playing in Post Op?

4. What does Potter order Charles to eat?

5. Whose oak-leaf clusters does Capt. Rockingham use?

EPISODE 10.15 "Pressure Points"

Director: Charles S. Dubin
Written by: David Pollock and Elias Davis

SELECTED SUPPORTING CAST
Allan Arbus as Maj. Sidney Freedman
John O'Donnell as Capt. Schnelker

SYNOPSIS
Potter feels he's losing his touch as a surgeon.

1. What is Charles looking for on his hands and knees in the Swamp?

2. What kind of ammunition does Schnelker tell the surgeons to expect?

3. Who offers Sidney a sardine?

4. What song does Potter say he'll turn off when Sidney visits him?

5. With which three slapstick comedians does Sidney compare Hawkeye, BJ, and Charles?

6. With what of BJ's does Charles use to clean his knife?

7. Where does Potter tell Klinger to store the newly arrived blood?

8. Who informs Potter BJ, Charles, and Hawkeye are destroying the Swamp?

9. What are BJ and Hawkeye breaking over their heads when Potter and Klinger enter the Swamp?

10. Which New York club does Sidney say Western singers play?

11. Who made Potter want to be a doctor?

EPISODE 10.16 "Where There's a Will, There's a War"

Director: Alan Alda
Written by: David Pollock and Elias Davis

SELECTED SUPPORTING CAST
Larry Ward as Gen. Kratzer
Dennis Howard as Captain Rackley
James Emery as Corpsman

SYNOPSIS
At an aid station, Hawkeye writes his will.

1. Where is BJ spending his R&R?

2. Why does Battalion Aid need a surgeon?

3. Where specifically was the surgeon killed?

4. Who is Hawkeye's main beneficiary?

5. What does Hawkeye will to Charles?

6. What does Hawkeye will to Fr. Mulcahy?

7. What does Hawkeye leave to Margaret?

8. What does he will to Potter?

9. What is willed to Klinger?

10. What does Capt. Rackley ask Hawkeye before he leaves?

11. What does Hawkeye leave Erin Hunnicutt?

EPISODE 10.17 "Promotion Commotion"

Director: Charles S. Dubin
Written by: Dennis Koenig

SELECTED SUPPORTING CAST
John Matuszak as Cpl. Elmo Hitalski
Jeff Maxwell as Pvt. Igor Straminsky
Kellye Nakahara as Lt. Kelley Yamato
Jim Reid Boyce as Danielson

Some will recognize John Matuszak from his football career, mainly with the Oakland Raiders.

SYNOPSIS
BJ, Hawkeye and Charles are on the promotion recommendation board.

1. In the opening scene in the OR, what does BJ say is his night job?

2. Who teaches Danielson to tie fishing flies?

3. To where does Danielson tell the guys from his unit he's transferred?

4. To which rank is Klinger promoted to?

EPISODE 10.18 "Heroes"

Director: Nell Cox
Written by: Thad Mumford and Dan Wilcox

SELECTED SUPPORTING CAST
Earl Boen as Maj. Robert Hatch
Pat McNamara as "Gentleman Joe" Cavanaugh

SYNOPSIS
A boxing legend dies during a visit to the 4077.

1. Who is the most excited to meet Cavanaugh?

2. How many years does Mulcahy say it's been since he and Cavanaugh "met"?

3. What medical event does Cavanaugh suffer?

4. What does a reporter pester BJ about in the shower?

5. According to Mulcahy, who were his two heroes?

EPISODE 10.19 "Sons and Bowlers"

Director: Hy Averback
Written by: Elias Davis & David Pollock

SELECTED SUPPORTING CAST
Dick O'Neill as Col. Pitts
William Lucking as Sgt. Marty Urbancic

SYNOPSIS
Charles consoles Hawkeye as Mr. Pierce undergoes surgery back in the States.

1. Which song are the Marines singing in the O Club?

2. What complaint does Potter have about Mulcahy's bowling?

3. How does Charles refer to Hawkeye for the first time while they wait in Klinger's office?

4. To what do Hawkeye and Charles drink to in the O Club?

EPISODE 10.20 "Picture This"

Director: Burt Metcalfe
Written by: Karen Hall

SELECTED SUPPORTING CAST
Jeff Maxwell as Pvt. Igor Straminsky
John Fujioka as Peasant

SYNOPSIS
Col. Potter tries to paint a portrait of his bickering staff members.

1. Who is barefoot in the opening scene in the mess tent?

2. What song does Hawkeye sing in his new accommodations?

3. Who is using a mirror to check their hair during one of the painting sessions?

EPISODE 10.21 "That Darn Kid"

Director: David Ogden Stiers
Written by: Karen Hall

SELECTED SUPPORTING CAST
G.W. Bailey as Sgt. Luther Rizzo
John P. Ryan as Maj. Van Zandt

SYNOPSIS

A goat eats the 4077 payroll.

1. Over what object does Charles compete with BJ?

2. How much money does Hawkeye owe to the Army after the goat eats it?

3. Who does Charles get a loan from?

4. In what kind of glass does Charles ask Igor to put the grape Nehi?

SEASON ELEVEN

STARRING

Alan Alda as Capt. Benjamin Franklin "Hawkeye" Pierce

Mike Farrell as Capt. BJ Hunnicutt

Henry Morgan as Col. Sherman T. Potter

Loretta Swit as Maj. Margaret Houlihan

David Ogden Stiers as Maj. Charles Emerson Winchester III

Jamie Farr as Cpl. Max Klinger

William Christopher as Fr. Francis Mulcahy

Trivia answers for Season Eleven begin on page 339.

EPISODE 11.1 "Hey, Look Me Over"

Director: Susan Oliver
Written by: Alan Alda and Karen Hall

SELECTED SUPPORTING CAST
Kellye Nakahara as Lt. Kellye Yamato
Peggy Feury as Col. Bucholtz
Perry Lang as Sandler
Rita Wilson as Lt. Lacey

SYNOPSIS
Kellye has had enough of Hawkeye ignoring her.

1. What is the staff doing at the start of the episode?

2. Which instrument does Igor hand BJ in OR?

3. Who asks Charles if Winchesters are quick healers?

4. Who fixes the autoclave?

5. Who does Hawkeye dance with at the O Club?

6. Where does Kellye confront Hawkeye?

EPISODE 11.2 "Trick or Treatment"

Director: Charles S. Dubin
Written by: Dennis Koenig

SELECTED SUPPORTING CAST
George Wendt as Pvt. LaRoche
Andrew Clay as Cpl. Hrabosky

George Wendt would be best known for his role as Norm Peterson on TV's *Cheers*.

Andrew Clay would go on to become actor/comedian Andrew "Dice" Clay.

SYNOPSIS
Misadventures on Halloween at the 4077.

1. Which surgeon is on duty?

2. What does a Marine get stuck in his mouth?

3. Who does Hawkeye go as for Halloween?

EPISODE 11.3 "Foreign Affairs"

Director: Charles S. Dubin
Written by: David Pollock and Elias Davis

SELECTED SUPPORTING CAST
Jeffrey Tambor as Maj. Reddish
Melinda Mullins as Martine LeClerc
Soon-Teck Oh as Joon-Sung
Byron Chung as Lt. Chung-Wa Park

SYNOPSIS

Charles falls for a French woman from the Red Cross.

1. How much money does Maj. Reddish offer Lt. Park?

2. Which songwriter is Charles surprised to find Martine enjoys?

3. What reason does Charles give to Martine that their relationship can't continue?

4. What does Hawkeye jokingly tell Joon-Sung not to do in America?

EPISODE 11.4 "The Joker Is Wild"

Director: Burt Metcalfe
Written by: John Rappaport and Dennis Koenig

SELECTED SUPPORTING CAST
Clyde Kusatsu as Capt. Paul Yamato

SYNOPSIS
Hawkeye becomes increasingly paranoid at BJ's pranks on the staff.

1. What practical joke does BJ pull on Hawkeye in the opening scene?

2. By what term of endearment does Mulcahy refer to Trapper?

3. What animal does Charles find in his bunk?

4. What has replaced Potter's toothpaste?

5. From which MASH unit is Capt. Yamato?

6. What joke was played on Margaret?

7. How many gang wars does Klinger say he's survived?

8. What does Capt. Yamato say he owes BJ?

9. What has Hawkeye surrounded himself with when he sleeps?

EPISODE 11.5 "Who Knew?"

Director: Harry Morgan
Written by: Elias Davis and David Pollock

SELECTED SUPPORTING CAST
Kellye Nakahara as Lt. Kellye Yamato
Enid Kent as Lt. Bigelow
Joanne Thompson as Nurse Jo Ann

SYNOPSIS
A nurse who many consider distant dies suddenly.

1. Where does Klinger ask Charles to meet him?

2. Who breaks the news to the staff that Millie has died?

3. Who helps Fr. Mulcahy gather Millie's personal effects?

4. What does Hawkeye use to better understand Millie?

EPISODE 11.6 "Bombshells"

Director: Charles S. Dubin
Written by: Dan Wilcox and Thad Mumford

SELECTED SUPPORTING CAST
Gerald O'Loughlin as Gen. Franklin Schwerin
Allen Williams as Lt. Priore

SYNOPSIS
Free time leads to a harrowing experience for BJ.

1. Who starts the rumor that Marilyn Monroe is coming to the 4077?

2. What does BJ set out to do with Lt. Priore?

3. How many pieces is the Army band?

4. To which song does Potter want to find the sheet music?

5. Which famous baseball player does Hawkeye impersonate on the phone when trying to reach Marilyn?

6. What is Klinger holding when the staff is assembled for Marilyn's arrival?

7. Which medal does Schwerin award to BJ?

EPISODE 11.7 "Settling Debts"

Director: Michael Switzer
Written by: Thad Mumford and Dan Wilcox

SELECTED SUPPORTING CAST
Jeff East as Lt. Pavelich
Guy Boyd as Sgt. Lally

SYNOPSIS
The surgeons plan a surprise mortgage burning party for Col. Potter.

1. According to BJ, how does Mildred outrank him and Hawkeye?

2. What does Potter think Mildred bought?

3. Which two characters try to keep Potter from his tent?

4. With which kind of fence do the surgical staff decorate the interior of Potter's tent?

5. Which surgeon passes out in Potter's tent?

EPISODE 11.8 "The Moon Is Not Blue"

Director: Charles S. Dubin
Written by: Larry Balmagia

SELECTED SUPPORTING CAST
Hamilton Camp as Maj. Frankenheimer
Sandy Helberg as Cpl. Bannister
Larry Ward as Gen. Rothaker
Jeff Maxwell as Pvt. Igor Straminsky

SYNOPSIS
A wounded general declares prohibition at the 4077.

1. Who announces the camp is going dry?

2. What does Charles call the still?

3. What causes the conflict between Charles and Igor?

EPISODE 11.9 "Run for the Money"

Director: Nell Cox
Written by: Elias Davis and David Pollock (teleplay), Mike Farrell, Elias Davis and David Pollock (story)

SELECTED SUPPORTING CAST
Thomas Callaway as Capt. Sweeney
Barbara Tarbuck as Maj. Judy Parker
Phil Brock as Pvt. Walt Palmer

SYNOPSIS
Charles helps a wounded man with a speech impediment.

1. What does Hawkeye say he can bench press?

2. Which MASH unit does the 4077 compete against?

3. From which college is Mulcahy's hooded sweatshirt?

4. Where does Mulcahy say he's keeping the winnings?

EPISODE 11.10 "U.N., the Night, and the Music"

Director: Harry Morgan
Written by: Elias Davis and David Pollock

SELECTED SUPPORTING CAST
George Innes as Dr. Randolph Kent
Dennis Holahan as Per Johannsen
Kavi Raz as Capt. Rammurti Lal

It may interest the reader to note that Loretta Swit would later marry Dennis Holahan.

SYNOPSIS
Delegates from the U.N. visit the camp.

1. From where does Charles say his brandy is from?

2. In who does Johannsen confide in regarding his condition?

3. Who is Col. Potter and Capt. Lal meditating with when Hawkeye comes looking for Potter?

4. In which direction does a meditating Hawkeye fall when Dr. Kent reveals his roots?

EPISODE 11.11 "Strange Bedfellows"

Director: Mike Farrell
Written by: Karen Hall

SELECTED SUPPORTING CAST
Dennis Dugan as Robert "Bob" Wilson

SYNOPSIS
Col. Potter discovers his son-in-law has had an affair.

1. Who comes to visit Potter?

2. What device do Hawkeye and BJ use to reveal Charles's snoring to him?

3. Where is the Imperial Hotel located?

4. What's Fr. Mulcahy working on when Potter comes to his tent?

5. Who does Charles talk to about his snoring?

6. Who is talking in their sleep at the end of the episode?

EPISODE 11.12 "Say No More"

Director: Charles S. Dubin
Written by: John Rappaport

SELECTED SUPPORTING CAST
John Anderson as Gen. Addison Collins
Michael Horton as Lt. Curt Collins

SYNOPSIS
The badly wounded son of a general is visited by his father.

1. Where is the lecture taking place?

2. Which doctor does Margaret see about her laryngitis?

3. Which Marx Brother does BJ refer to regarding Margaret's hair?

4. What action does Margaret mime to Kellye in Post Op?

5. Who breaks the news of his son's passing away to the general?

6. What does Margaret give to Charles at the end of the episode?

EPISODE 11.13 "Friends and Enemies"

Director: Jamie Farr
Written by: Karen Hall

SELECTED SUPPORTING CAST
John McLiam as Col. Woody Cooke
Roy Goldman as Roy Goldman

SYNOPSIS
An old friend of Potter's causes casualties.

1. Who runs over BJ's toe with a cart in Post Op?

2. What does BJ do to sabotage Charles's phonograph?

3. Where does Charles try to play his records?

4. Which color is the fan Charles gives to Margaret?

EPISODE 11.14 "Give and Take"

Director: Charles S. Dubin
Written by: Dennis Koenig

SELECTED SUPPORTING CAST
Craig Wasson as Pvt. Kurland
G.W. Bailey as Sgt. Luther Rizzo

SYNOPSIS

A wounded American soldier and an enemy soldier he badly wounded share space in Post Op.

1. Who does Charles ask first for a donation?

2. Which poet does Margaret admire?

3. What chore does BJ ask Margaret to do in exchange for him taking over as charity officer?

4. What does Klinger pass out to the patients in Post Op?

5. What liquor does Klinger tell Mulcahy he has?

EPISODE 11.15 "As Time Goes By"

Director: Burt Metcalfe
Written by: Dan Wilcox and Thad Mumford

SELECTED SUPPORTING CAST
G.W. Bailey as Sgt. Luther Rizzo
Rosalind Chao as Soon-Lee
Kellye Nakahara as Lt. Kellye Yamato

SYNOPSIS

Margaret wants to bury a time capsule honoring the 4077.

1. Which American city does Charles ridicule in the O Club?

2. Where does Rizzo get the hand grenade?

3. What is the first thing Hawkeye gives to Margaret for her time capsule?

4. What article of Radar's does Hawkeye give to Margaret?

5. What item of Col. Blake's does BJ give to Margaret?

EPISODE 11.16 "Goodbye, Farewell, and Amen"

Director: Alan Alda

Written by: Alan Alda, Burt Metcalfe, John Rappaport, Dan Wilcox, Thad Mumford, Elias Davis, David Pollock and Karen Hall

SELECTED SUPPORTING CAST
Allan Arbus as Maj. Sidney Freedman
G.W. Bailey as Sgt. Luther Rizzo
Rosalind Chao as Soon-Lee
Kellye Nakahara as Lt. Kellye Yamato
Jeff Maxwell as Pvt. Igor Straminsky

SYNOPSIS
The Korean War ends, and the 4077 staff faces their futures. The Series Finale.

1. In which ward is Hawkeye located?

2. Who speaks the first line?

3. What color is the robe Hawkeye is wearing?

4. What do the staff use for volleyball netting at the beach?

5. Who is the first person Hawkeye talks to on the phone?

6. What is the rank of the MP guarding the POWs?

7. In which stateside hospital does Charles want to work?

8. What kind of transportation are the Chinese musicians using when they encounter Charles?

9. How many musicians are there?

10. Where in camp do they put the musicians?

11. What color does BJ paint his motorcycle?

12. Which composer's music do the musicians play that gets Charles's attention?

13. Who lets the POWs out of their pen during the mortar attack on the compound?

14. Who comes to visit Hawkeye?

15. What kind of game do Hawkeye, Sidney and BJ play?

16. Which nurse assists Hawkeye in his first surgery back at the 4077?

17. What wakes Rizzo from his nap?

18. Where does Rizzo hide during the attack?

19. Who moves the tank into the dump?

20. What is the reason for the bug out?

21. What kind of dress does Klinger try to give to Soon-Lee?

22. What sports game do 4077 staffers play with the Korean children?

23. Who greets Sidney when he arrives at the 4077?

24. What do the staff give to BJ and a Korean child?

25. What does Hawkeye tell Sidney returning to surgery is like?

26. Who's first off the bus when they return to what's left of the 4077 after the fire?

27. What does BJ refuse to say to Hawkeye?

28. What does Charles do when he discovers the fate of the Chinese musicians?

29. What are the doctors doing when the shelling stops?

30. Who does Klinger ask to be his best man?

31. Who is dabbing their eyes at Klinger and Soon-Lee's wedding?

32. Who is the last person Klinger says goodbye to?

33. What does Charles give to Margaret?

34. In what kind of vehicle does Charles leave?

35. What does Hawkeye and BJ do to say goodbye to Col. Potter?

36. How does Hawkeye leave the 4077?

37. Which of the staffers is the last to leave the compound?

38. What message does BJ leave for Hawkeye in stones on the chopper pad?

ANSWERS

SEASON ONE

EPISODE 1.1 "Pilot"

1. "A hundred years ago."
2. Football.
3. His left.
4. Two.
5. "Red."
6. Twelve.
7. Ten bucks.
8. What color is the military scrip Hawkeye and Trapper count?
9. What does Frank stumble over after getting thrown out of the Swamp?
10. A white panama.
11. Gen. Hammond.
12. "Over eighteen hundred bucks."
13. "Ugh… the mummy strikes!"
14. Canada.
15. His right.

EPISODE 1.2 "To Market, To Market"

1. Oak.
2. Henry.

3. MacArthur.
4. South Korea.
5. $10,000.00.
6. A three-star general.
7. The top comes off.
8. "Just for being you."
9. They detach an entire wall.
10. O'Brien.
11. If he's sending it out to be waxed.

EPISODE 1.3 "Requiem for a Lightweight"

1. The flowers he just planted.
2. Packing.
3. "Dr. Jekyll and Dr. Jekyll."
4. "In school."
5. Radar.
6. A glass stomach.
7. Frank's.
8. Ether.
9. Sergeant.
10. Kid Doctor.
11. Radar.

EPISODE 1.4 "Chief Surgeon Who?"

1. A guitar and a martini.
2. A form letter.
3. Two.
4. Not once.
5. Hawkeye.

6. A plunger.
7. Two.
8. Fungus face.
9. Smoking one of Henry's cigars and drinking his brandy.
10. Klinger.
11. A worm.

EPISODE 1.5 "The Moose"

1. Sergeant.
2. "Gooks."
3. A flush.
4. Reading.
5. "Happy like hell!"
6. Trapper.
7. "Part moose, part yo-yo."
8. "Yes, I am."
9. Benny.

EPISODE 1.6 "Yankee Doodle Doctor"

1. Dancing.
2. Lt. Bricker.
3. James Cagney.
4. Romeo.
5. Frank.
6. From inside the stove.
7. Groucho and Harpo Marx, respectively.
8. A saw.

EPISODE 1.7 "Bananas, Crackers, and Nuts"

1. The Operating Room.
2. Steak and potatoes.
3. The size of a basketball.
4. Seven days.
5. Tokyo.
6. Scrubs.
7. Liver from a North Korean.
8. Frank.
9. Blue.
10. Trapper.

EPISODE 1.8 "Cowboy"

1. His shoulder.
2. His ears.
3. Twenty-nine.
4. Ho-Jon.
5. A driverless jeep.
6. "Boom."
7. All of it.
8. His chair.
9. Purple Rider.
10. Reno.
11. A jeep backfire.

EPISODE 1.9 "Henry Please Come Home"

1. "Cocktails for Two."

2. Ginger.
3. Applaud.
4. Radar.
5. The still.
6. Push him into a chopper blade.
7. Radar.

EPISODE 1.10 "I Hate a Mystery"

1. A sterling silver frame.
2. Her hairbrushes.
3. His watch.
4. His swizzle stick.
5. Soot.
6. Hawkeye's footlocker.
7. Radar.
8. Ho-Jon.
9. To bribe the border guards to let his family through to the south.

EPISODE 1.11 "Germ Warfare"

1. AB-.
2. The Swamp.
3. Typhoid Mary.
4. Lt. Dish.
5. Checkers.

EPISODE 1.12 "Dear Dad"

1. Vermont.
2. A jeep. Piece by piece.
3. A football.
4. Trapper.
5. A lollipop.
6. A bandanna.
7. A hand grenade.
8. Pudding.
9. Hawkeye.
10. Four.

EPISODE 1.13 "Edwina"

1. "For She's a Jolly Good Fellow."
2. The salt.
3. They draw straws.
4. "Gravy that didn't make it."
5. Trapper and Radar.
6. Salutes.
7. Black.

EPISODE 1.14 "Love Story"

1. He isn't eating.
2. Three.
3. "Ahhh, *Bach!*"
4. Hot Lips.
5. Hawkeye and Trapper.

6. "Uncle."

EPISODE 1.15 "Tuttle"

1. Frank.
2. Fangs.
3. Battle Creek, MI.
4. Auburn.
5. "I think I'm in love."
6. Hawkeye.
7. Radar.
8. Major Murdock.

EPISODE 1.16 "The Ringbanger"

1. "Knock on the 'condemned' sign and come in."
2. A cane.
3. His right.
4. Never being sick.
5. Twice.

Episode 1.17 "Sometimes You Hear the Bullet"

1. "Pennsylvania 6-5000."
2. Corporal.
3. Kisses him.
4. *You Never Hear the Bullet.*

EPISODE 1.18 "Dear Dad... Again"

1. A wedding dress.
2. The mess tent.
3. A high school final.
4. A martini (a double).
5. His brain won't get any air.
6. Sergeant.
7. Schwartz.

EPISODE 1.19 "The Longjohn Flap"

1. A chair.
2. He loses them in a poker game.
3. A pair of socks.
4. Appendicitis.

EPISODE 1.20 "The Army/Navy Game"

1. Notre Dame.
2. His wife, then-named Mildred (it would later become Lorraine).
3. Frank.
4. He faints.
5. Hawkeye.
6. The Navy.
7. 21-20.
9. Wink.
10. Trapper.

11. Counter-clockwise.
12. A propaganda bomb.

EPISODE 1.21 "Sticky Wicket"

1. Coffee.
2. An ace-high flush.
3. His boot.
4. Frank insults his ability as a surgeon.
5. The mess tent.
6. The kitchen sink.

EPISODE 1.22 "Major Frank C. Dobbs"

1. Radar.
2. With extra fat.
3. *Just Plain MacArthur.*

EPISODE 1.23 "Ceasefire"

1. Gen. Clayton.
2. Toilet paper.
3. "Compliments of a friend."
4. They get *very* drunk.

EPISODE 1.24 "Showtime"

1. Reading a book.
2. It sprays in Hawkeye's face.

3. Dill pickles.
4. Radar.

SEASON TWO

EPISODE 2.1 "Divided We Stand"

1. An angel of mercy.
2. Brandy.
3. The men's showers.
4. Someone's appendix.
5. Filing the skeleton's fingernails.
6. Binoculars.

EPISODE 2.2 "Five O'Clock Charlie"

1. Five.
2. An anti-aircraft gun.
3. Charlie bombs his jeep.
4. Three.
5. A golf club.
6. Four dozen.
7. Drinking from an IV tube.
8. Four.
9. *The Wall Street Journal*.

EPISODE 2.3 "Radar's Report"

1. An adding machine.
2. AB-.
3. Klinger.
4. A stethoscope.
5. Coffee.
6. "What's your name, honey?"
7. Hot Lips.
8. Practicing his golf game.

EPISODE 2.4 "For the Good of the Outfit"

1. "As American as apple pie and napalm."
2. Frank.
3. He has a briefcase.
4. He has a drink.

EPISODE 2.5 "Dr. Pierce and Mr. Hyde"

1. Thunder.
2. Twenty hours.
3. A wheelchair.
4. A clothesline.
5. Reading a comic book.
6. "Who's responsible?"
7. Frank.
8. The officer's latrine.

EPISODE 2.6 "Kim"

1. Frank.
2. Catch.
3. His teddy bear.
4. *Goldilocks and the Three Bears.*
5. B for "Boom."
6. O'Brien.
7. Trapper.

EPISODE 2.7 "LIP (Local Indigenous Personnel)"

1. In an ambulance.
2. John Wayne.
3. Klinger.
4. Frank's.
5. Blackmail him.
6. Klinger.

EPISODE 2.8 "The Trial of Henry Blake"

1. Ping-pong.
2. The Style Right Show Company.
3. Klinger.
4. A hang-glider.
5. "A big red bird with fuzzy pink feet."
6. Two.

EPISODE 2.9 "Dear Dad... Three"

1. Cards (Gin).
2. Hot Lips.
3. She said she liked him.
4. Marion.
5. Trapper.

EPISODE 2.10 "The Sniper"

1. Pearl grips.
2. The showers.
3. Seven.
4. Hawkeye.
5. By taking cover behind an arriving ambulance.
6. Six.
7. His left arm.
8. Trapper.
9. Twice as long.
10. The mess tent.
11. He hangs it on the skeleton.
12. Camouflage netting.

EPISODE 2.11 "Carry On, Hawkeye"

1. Trapper.
2. Frank's Bible.
3. "Intelligent octopus!"
4. Mr. and Mrs. Judas.
5. His wife (or Nancy, his secretary).

EPISODE 2.12 "The Incubator"

1. A beer can.
2. Coffee
3. Sunglasses.
4. Four.
5. Be set for rare.

EPISODE 2.13 "Deal Me Out"

1. Sidney.
2. 1800 hours.
3. He takes their robes.
4. Red and blue.
5. Because one of the sandwiches moved.
6. His wife.
7. He refuses to go outside without a bulletproof couch.
8. The showers.
9. Trapper.

EPISODE 2.14 "Hot Lips and Empty Arms"

1. Bimbo, a stuffed dog.
2. Alcohol.
3. Scotch.
4. "Pete."
5. Trapper.
6. A load of B1.

EPISODE 2.15 "Officers Only"

1. Radar.
2. Pregnant.
3. A case of pipe cleaners.
4. They stand at attention.
5. A pulpit.
6. A Shirley Temple.
7. 32.

EPISODE 2.16 "Henry in Love"

1. Hot cocoa.
2. Red, white, and blue.
3. A towel.
4. His hair.
5. Frank.
6. A jet flying overhead.
7. The dog.

EPISODE 2.17 "For Want of a Boot"

1. 5,000 diapers and 5 pairs of rubber pants.
2. Frank's birthday card.
3. Throw a birthday party for him.
4. A riding crop.
5. His golf bag.

EPISODE 2.18 "Operation Noselift"

1. Discipline.
2. "Stosh."
3. Radar.
4. The women's showers.

EPISODE 2.19 "The Chosen People"

1. An egg.
2. "Quac" (or "Quack").
3. "Holy cow!"
4. Fire a few shots over their heads.
5. Radar.
6. Two.

EPISODE 2.20 "As You Were"

1. Radar.
2. Washing his feet.
3. A crate.
4. Gorilla suits.
5. His tan.
6. Three.

EPISODE 2.21 "Crisis"

1. Red alert.
2. Bingo.

3. A ham.
4. Hawkeye.
5. A brassiere.
6. Klinger.
7. The skeleton and the phone.

EPISODE 2.22 "George"

1. "I've Got You Under My Skin."
2. He sings louder.
3. Mulcahy.
4. Checkers.
5. His brain.
6. A Nativity scene.

EPISODE 2.23 "Mail Call"

1. A sweater.
2. Balance her checkbook.
3. His upper lip disappears.
4. Pioneer Aviation.
5. Trapper.
6. "Pioneer Aviation!"
7. A table knife.
8. Eight o'clock.

EPISODE 2.24 "A Smattering of Intelligence"

1. A wooden swab.
2. Four.

3. Two.
4. The X-ray machine.
5. Mary.
6. He stands in the office doorway smoking a cigarette.

SEASON THREE

EPISODE 3.1 "The General Flipped at Dawn"

1. The cesspool.
2. Aaron Burr.
3. Trapper, Hawkeye, and Klinger.
4. The Swine Brothers.
5. Two.
6. The hairs in his nose.
7. Marjorie.
8. His shirt pocket.
9. The ukulele.
10. Twenty minutes.

EPISODE 3.2 "Rainbow Bridge"

1. Klinger.
2. Henry.
3. Nine.
4. Fifty.
5. Margaret.
6. Five. (Hawkeye, Trapper, Frank, Radar, and Klinger.)

7. A jeep.
8. "What the hell is *that?*"

EPISODE 3.3 "Officer of the Day"

1. Igor.
2. A gun.
3. White flags.
4. "Olivia de Havilland."
5. His watch.
6. Klinger.
7. Five.
8. The pinstripes are horizontal rather than vertical.

EPISODE 3.4 "Iron Guts Kelly"

1. A piece of gum.
2. Three.
3. Igor.
4. Shaving his head.
5. A general's star.

EPISODE 3.5 "O.R."

1. His fingernail brush.
2. Ethiopia.
3. *Blood and Sand.*
4. Trapper.
5. Klinger.
6. Orange juice.

7. Trapper.

EPISODE 3.6 "Springtime"

1. Klinger.
2. Hawkeye.
3. A wedding dress.

EPISODE 3.7 "Check-Up"

1. Antacid.
2. Hawkeye.
3. An anchor.
4. Frank.
5. Toledo.
6. "Who died?"
7. Klinger.
8. "America the Beautiful."

EPISODE 3.8 "Life with Father"

1. Playing catch with a football.
2. The *Essex*.
3. A lightbox and/or a microscope.
4. He hits himself in the arm.

EPISODE 3.9 "Alcoholics Unanimous"

1. Radar.

2. Klinger.
3. Brandy.
4. Leviticus 10.
5. One of the stained-glass windows.

EPISODE 3.10 "There's Nothing Like a Nurse"

1. Hungover.
2. Radar.
3. "At least two feet."
4. His hair trimmings.
5. They park a jeep over him.

EPISODE 3.11 "Adam's Ribs"

1. Liver and fish.
2. Radar.
3. Forty pounds, and one gallon.
4. The coleslaw.

EPISODE 3.12 "A Full Rich Day"

1. Lt. LeClerq (from Luxembourg).
2. *The Last of the Mohicans* by James Fenimore Cooper.
3. The Turkish soldier.
4. His manservant.
5. Radar's.
6. "Damn good Joe."

EPISODE 3.13 "Mad Dogs and Servicemen"

1. A turtle.
2. Henry.
3. Boston.

EPISODE 3.14 "Private Charles Lamb"

1. A skunk.
2. Sixteen.
3. A hairball.
4. A toothpick.
5. A boot.
6. Frank.

EPISODE 3.15 "Bombed"

1. Mulcahy.
2. She slaps Margaret back.
3. Trapper.
4. Sanchez.

EPISODE 3.16 "Bulletin Board"

1. Fall asleep.
2. "Kiss me."
3. A pillow.
4. Shirley Temple.
5. She pops it.

6. She assaults him.

EPISODE 3.17 "The Consultant"

1. A Zombie.
2. World War None.
3. England.
4. Trapper and Margaret.

EPISODE 3.18 "House Arrest"

1. Frank snaps him with a towel.
2. A bar of soap.
3. A prisoner-of-war package.
4. New glasses.
5. Two.

EPISODE 3.19 "Aid Station"

1. Margaret.
2. He marks the levels.
3. Radar.
4. Margaret.
5. Snow White.
6. "God Bless America."
7. "The Caissons Go Rolling Along."

EPISODE 3.20 "Love and Marriage"

1. Radar.
2. One of Hawkeye's chips.
3. One.
4. Parker Brothers.
5. Hot water.

EPISODE 3.21 "Big Mac"

1. A hysterectomy.
2. Smile or tell MacArthur he's pregnant.
3. Flowers.
4. Radar.
5. The Statue of Liberty.

EPISODE 3.22 "Payday"

1. A slice of bread.
2. $10.00
3. Mulcahy.
4. Losing.

EPISODE 3.23 "White Gold"

1. Three.
2. A rabbi.
3. He bangs his pipe on the stove.

EPISODE 3.24 "Abyssinia, Henry"

1. His dad had a stroke.
2. A rectal thermometer.
3. Carmen Miranda.
4. Come back and kick his butt.
5. The Sea of Japan.

SEASON FOUR

EPISODE 4.1 "Welcome to Korea"

1. In the filing cabinet (under "B").
2. Spring.
3. Hawkeye.
4. His uniform.
5. Radar.
6. Hawkeye.
7. Ten.
8. Corporal Captain.
9. A grape Nehi.
10. Mill Valley, California.
11. Radar.
12. His hat.
13. Radar.
14. He salutes it.

EPISODE 4.2 "Change of Command"

1. He holds his breath.
2. He honks his jeep's horn.
3. Frank.
4. Two years.
5. Guam.
6. His still blew up.
7. "Stud."

EPISODE 4.3 "It Happened One Night"

1. A golf ball.
2. Socks.
3. "Caribbean."
4. His shoulder.
5. 18.
6. B+.
7. A can of beans.
8. Margaret's.

EPISODE 4.4 "The Late Captain Pierce"

1. Klinger.
2. BJ.
3. Digger's.
4. Popcorn.
5. Carrots.
6. *1984*.

EPISODE 4.5 "Hey, Doc"

1. A swimmer's cap.
2. A houseplant.
3. Eight years old.
4. Frank.
5. He shoots it.

EPISODE 4.6 "The Bus"

1. Radar.
2. 100 yards.
3. A fighter jet.
4. Chocolate.
5. Frank.
6. Frank.
7. Radar.
8. The Korean soldier.

EPISODE 4.7 "Dear Mildred"

1. He uses it as a shim.
2. 27.
3. "Squirrely."
4. Dysentery.
5. Hawkeye.
6. Wood.
7. Pig Latin.
8. The Motor Pool.

EPISODE 4.8 "The Kids"

1. He kisses her hand.
2. An egg shell fragment.
3. "Mama-san."
4. The newborn baby.
5. His teddy bear.

EPISODE 4.9 "Quo Vadis, Captain Chandler?"

1. Hawkeye.
2. Cowardice and blasphemy.
3. The Shadow.
4. Under his shirt.
5. Godzilla.
6. His loyalty oath.
7. Mary.
8. Walter.
9. Moses.

EPISODE 4.10 "Dear Peggy"

1. Embalmer's school.
2. Margaret.
3. A "crazy agnostic."
4. Going to church.
5. Three.
6. A raft.
7. Chess.

EPISODE 4.11 "Of Moose and Men"

1. Bourbon.
2. His right.
3. One fourth.
4. Battleship.
5. His wife.

EPISODE 4.12 "Soldier of the Month"

1. Klinger
2. Klinger.
3. Hawkeye and BJ.
4. Four.
5. Father Mulcahy.
6. Karate.

EPISODE 4.13 "The Gun"

1. Sleeping.
2. John Wayne.
3. BJ and Hawkeye.
4. 16.
5. A football injury.

EPISODE 4.14 "Mail Call...Again"

1. James Cagney.
2. A pillow.

3. Two.
4. Margaret.
5. A chair.
6. Ranger.

EPISODE 4.15 "The Price of Tomato Juice"

1. A three-day pass.
2. His wife.
3. BJ.

EPISODE 4.16 "Dear Ma"

1. Because he knows she can't read fast.
2. His boot is tied to a table leg.
3. A guinea pig.
4. A hand mirror.
5. BJ.
6. Red nail polish.

EPISODE 4.17 "Der Tag"

1. A gopher.
2. Eddie Bertolucci.
3. Cough drops.
4. About $200.
5. Drums (with brushes).

EPISODE 4.18 "Hawkeye"

1. Three (one on the way).
2. Battery acid.
3. A surgical glove.
4. "Some Enchanted Evening."
5. Laurence Olivier.

EPISODE 4.19 "Some 38th Parallels"

1. A violin.
2. "Carmen."
3. Maj. Houlihan.
4. $5.
5. Crying.
6. Horseshoes.
7. The camp's garbage.
8. A helmet.

EPISODE 4.20 "The Novocaine Mutiny"

1. "Know Your Enema."
2. Three.
3. Having a spelling bee.
4. He was hit by a door.

EPISODE 4.21 "Smilin' Jack"

1. Three.

2. Yellow.
3. He takes their picture.
4. Potter.
5. Dangerous Dan.
6. Fried chicken.
7. "Each and every one."

EPISODE 4.22 "The More I See You"

1. Changing a lightbulb.
2. Toilet paper.
3. "Pure poison."
4. A turtle.
5. A printing error ("Thou *shall* commit adultery").

EPISODE 4.23 "Deluge"

1. Vietnam.
2. Looking through his broken glasses.
3. She wasn't allowed to get a crew cut.
4. A cat.
5. Klinger and Radar.

EPISODE 4.24 "The Interview"

1. The dictionary.
2. Earthworms.
3. Three.
4. The nurses.
5. His family.

SEASON FIVE

EPISODE 5.1 "Bug Out"

1. Three.
2. "That's where Maj. Burns sits."
3. Ten.
4. Alice.
5. Three.
6. A banana.
7. Potter.
8. Horseback.
9. Klinger's dresses.

EPISODE 5.2 "Margaret's Engagement"

1. He rips off both doors.
2. A hand grenade.
3. Radar.

EPISODE 5.3 "Out of Sight, Out of Mind"

1. Four.
2. A three-star general.
3. A duck call.
4. A cane.

EPISODE 5.4 "Lt. Radar O'Reilly"

1. A whip.
2. "You Oughta Be in Pictures."
3. Klinger.

EPISODE 5.5 "The Nurses"

1. A lei.
2. Tony.
3. A red scarf.

EPISODE 5.6 "The Abduction of Margaret Houlihan"

1. Basketball.
2. BJ.
3. A showgirl.
4. His teddy bear.
5. About a dozen.

EPISODE 5.7 "Dear Sigmund"

1. Flippers.
2. Hawkeye and BJ.
3. A severe Geritol deficiency.
4. Foxholes.
5. A basin of (presumably hot) water.

EPISODE 5.8 "Mulcahy's War"

1. Corporal Cupcake.
2. Igor.
3. His Tom Mix pocketknife.
4. The dropper from his eyedrops.
5. Grace.

EPISODE 5.9 "The Korean Surgeon"

1. Hawkeye.
2. Radar and Klinger.
3. Captain.
4. Burial plots.

EPISODE 5.10 "Hawkeye Get Your Gun"

1. Dig latrines.
2. A gypsy.
3. Cards (two low cards out of four).
4. Water.
5. Hawkeye.
6. "Sleep."
7. A straight.
8. Five.
9. Five.

EPISODE 5.11 "The Colonel's Horse"

1. The Abbott and Costello Look-Alike Contest.
2. Zorro.
3. Radar.
4. BJ.
5. Hawkeye.

EPISODE 5.12 "Exorcism"

1. His aftershave.
2. Friday, the 13th.
3. A horseshoe.
4. Radar.
5. Red.

EPISODE 5.13 "Hawk's Nightmare"

1. A French hooker.
2. "Playing" basketball.
3. Two years.
4. He'll get lockjaw.

EPISODE 5.14 "The Most Unforgettable Characters"

1. A squirrel.
2. Frank's.
3. Flies.

4. Guard.
5. BJ.
6. Radar.

EPISODE 5.15 "38 Across"

1. The *Essex*.
2. A jeep.
3. A goat.

EPISODE 5.16 "Ping Pong"

1. Yellow.
2. Two.
3. Horseshoes.
4. Radar.
5. Margaret.
6. Blue.

EPISODE 5.17 "End Run"

1. Three.
2. Mashed potatoes.
3. Radar.
4. Margaret.

EPISODE 5.18 "Hanky Panky"

1. Radar.
2. He gets in her way in the kitchen.
3. She thinks he's dying.
4. The Toledo Strangler.
5. A double hernia.

EPISODE 5.19 "Hepatitis"

1. A roll of toilet paper.
2. Hawkeye.
3. Fig Newtons and Scotch. ("They're great if you dip 'em!")

EPISODE 5.20 "The General's Practitioner"

1. Three.
2. BJ.
3. "No neck, one eyebrow."
4. Frank.
5. His chewing gum.

EPISODE 5.21 "Movie Tonight"

1. Frank.
2. One sleeve is longer than the other.
3. Her whip.
4. *My Darling Clementine*.

5. "The Tennessee Waltz."
6. Radar.
7. Margaret.

EPISODE 5.22 "Souvenirs"

1. Pontius Pilate.
2. Margaret.
3. Margaret.
4. Drake.
5. 22.

EPISODE 5.23 "Post Op"

1. Margaret.
2. Hawkeye.
3. Frank.

EPISODE 5.24 "Margaret's Marriage"

1. "Stormy Weather."
2. Mulcahy.
3. A wedding dress.
4. Radar.
5. His Uncle Ed.
6. Strong enough to kill his horse.
7. Klinger.
8. Frank, who tosses it to Kellye.
9. "Goodbye, Margaret."

SEASON SIX

EPISODE 6.1 "Fade Out, Fade In"

1. 0400.
2. Mulcahy.
3. Cribbage.
4. Four, including the one that hits the jeep.
5. Through the window.
6. A cart.
7. Her alarm clock.
8. Gin.
9. Two.
10. He throws it out the door.
11. A snake.
12. Mozart.

EPISODE 6.2 "Fallen Idol"

1. Mortar fire.
2. "Over the Rainbow."
3. Charles.
4. Smiles.
5. Mulcahy.
6. Rosie's.
7. A salute.

EPISODE 6.3 "Last Laugh"

1. "The Alphabet Song."

2. A camel.
3. A hat.

EPISODE 6.4 "War of Nerves"

1. Chinese.
2. Margaret.
3. That he really *is* going crazy.
4. *I Love Lucy.*
5. The Army Cookbook.
6. Charles's cot.

EPISODE 6.5 "The Winchester Tapes"

1. Charles.
2. Soup from the mess tent.
3. Cake sent from Peg.
4. A rubber chicken.
5. A rubber chicken.

EPISODE 6.6 "The Light That Failed"

1. Boris Karloff.
2. Sergeant.
3. *The Rooster Crowed at Midnight.*
4. Abigail Porterfield.
5. Charles.
6. Curare.
7. "There's no limelight."

EPISODE 6.7 "In Love and War"

1. Pneumonia.
2. A mile.
3. French.
4. "A cute vulture."

EPISODE 6.8 "Change Day"

1. From blue to red.
2. Ten cents on the dollar.
3. French.
4. The Navy.

EPISODE 6.9 "Images"

1. Rembrandt.
2. A beer.
3. A teddy bear.

EPISODE 6.10 "The MASH Olympics"

1. Four.
2. Sixty-seven.
3. A bedpan.
4. The Yellow Blackbirds.
5. The Pink Elephants.
6. 5 to 5.
7. The Obstacle Course.

EPISODE 6.11 "The Grim Reaper"

1. BJ.
2. His "Diary of Death."
3. It's too small.
4. Potter.
5. Charles.

EPISODE 6.12 "Comrades in Arms: Part One"

1. Six.
2. "We Never Close."
3. He kicks it.
4. Four.
5. A maid.
6. His right.

EPISODE 6.13 "Comrades in Arms: Part 2"

1. Crackers and jam.
2. Potter.
3. BJ.
4. A MASH compass.
5. Klinger.
6. Hank.

EPISODE 6.14 "The Merchant of Korea"

1. Close a patient for him.

2. He hoses them down.
3. $20.

EPISODE 6.15 "The Smell of Music"

1. The French horn.
2. A pair of his used socks.
3. "A sawed-off tuba."

EPISODE 6.16 "Patent 4077"

1. "Over hill, over dale, our love will never fail."
2. Charles.
3. Zale.
4. His nose.
5. Hawkeye's.
6. $10.

EPISODE 6.17 "Tea and Empathy"

1. "Get out."
2. England.
3. Red.
4. His skirt.

EPISODE 6.18 "Your Hit Parade"

1. Double Cranko.
2. Hawkeye.

3. Klinger.
4. "Sentimental Journey."
5. Potter.
6. Too much rice.

EPISODE 6.19 "What's Up, Doc?"

1. Sherlock Holmes.
2. Fluffy.
3. Yale.

EPISODE 6.20 "Mail Call Three"

1. His pen.
2. Charles.
3. Hawkeye and Mulcahy.
4. BJ.
5. Klinger.

EPISODE 6.21 "Temporary Duty"

1. The Terrible Twins.
2. BJ's.
3. Cowboy hat and cowboy boots.
4. Chess.

EPISODE 6.22 "Potter's Retirement"

1. One year.

2. Green cough syrup.
3. Klinger.
4. Hawkeye.

EPISODE 6.23 "Dr. Winchester and Mr. Hyde"

1. *The Catcher in the Rye.*
2. Sluggo.
3. Daisy.
4. His footlocker.

EPISODE 6.24 "Major Topper"

1. Rosemary Clooney.
2. Charles.
3. Father Mulcahy.
4. Ten.
5. Two.
6. Audrey Hepburn.

SEASON SEVEN

EPISODE 7.1 "Commander Pierce"

1. Laughing.
2. A cringing chicken.
3. Green.
4. Flowers.

EPISODE 7.2 "Peace on Us"

1. An operating table.
2. She kicks one of the doors down.
3. Two.
4. Gastritis.
5. A moustache.

EPISODE 7.3 "Lil"

1. 22 years.
2. A bottle of Scotch.
3. Radar.
4. "Harrigan."

EPISODE 7.4 "Our Finest Hour Part One and Part Two"

1. Radar.
2. His own room.
3. His wife's cooking.
4. Mulcahy.

EPISODE 7.5 "The Billfold Syndrome"

1. Cleaning up trash.
2. The heart.
3. Military Solitaire.

EPISODE 7.6 "None Like It Hot"

1. His hat.
2. Abercrombie & Fitch
3. Hawkeye.
4. Incense.
5. The rubber duck.
6. *"Nyet."*
7. Strawberry.

EPISODE 7.7 "They Call the Wind Korea"

1. His saddle.
2. Red.
3. "Rock-Bye Baby."
4. Bigelow.
5. Greece.
6. Seven.
7. Cosmetics.
8. A funny nose and glasses.

EPISODE 7.8 "Major Ego"

1. Orange juice.
2. Hawkeye and BJ.
3. Yellow.
4. BJ.
5. Dorothy.

EPISODE 7.9 "Baby, It's Cold Outside"

1. Pack wolves.
2. Green.
3. Fur-lined gloves.
4. The latrine.
5. It makes his face break out.
6. "Camel Nose."

EPISODE 7.10 "Point of View"

1. Eight.
2. His throat.
3. BJ and Radar.
4. She tries to cover his eyes during anesthesia.

EPISODE 7.11 "Dear Comrade"

1. Pretending to conduct and lip-sync along to the music he's listening to.
2. A novelty wig.
3. "A capitalist fool."
4. The cesspool.
5. Concrete.

EPISODE 7.12 "Out of Gas"

1. Poker.
2. The 8063rd.

3. Mulcahy and Charles.
4. Three.
5. Their truck.

EPISODE 7.13 "An Eye for a Tooth"

1. Polishing his saddle.
2. Lemon meringue.
3. Father Mulcahy.

EPISODE 7.14 "Dear Sis"

1. Christmas.
2. Mushrooms.
3. One of the cows on his mom's farm.
4. Charles.
5. Mulcahy.
6. A pair of pajamas for his teddy bear.
7. BJ.

EPISODE 7.15 "BJ Papa-San"

1. The ankle.
2. Isabella.
3. The roof.
4. Blitzen.
5. "Night and Day."
6. It gets a flat tire.

EPISODE 7.16 "Inga"

1. Bach.
2. Her ears.
3. Heart surgery.
4. A soggy piece of liver.

EPISODE 7.17 "The Price"

1. On horseback.
2. Pink.
3. Potter.
4. One of Klinger's dresses.
5. In Charles's cot.

EPISODE 7.18 "The Young and the Restless"

1. Hawkeye.
2. Radar.
3. Charles.
4. An ice pack.
5. His rank.

EPISODE 7.19 "Hot Lips is Back in Town"

1. Cory.
2. "Lullaby of Broadway."
3. Hawkeye and BJ.
4. Colonel.

5. Herself.

EPISODE 7.20 "C*A*V*E"

1. Under his desk.
2. "Eskimo Pie."
3. Potter and Charles.
4. The walls will cave in.
5. "Hi honey, I'm home!"
6. Mulcahy and Charles.
7. Joan of Arc.

EPISODE 7.21 "Rally 'Round the Flagg, Boys"

1. Bridge.
2. His finger.
3. A trash can.
4. Radar.
5. Charles.

EPISODE 7.22 "Preventative Medicine"

1. Illinois.
2. Their Purple Hearts.
3. A mug and shaving brush.
4. His appendix.

EPISODE 7.23 "A Night at Rosie's"

1. Two days.
2. Klinger.
3. Pretending to dance with someone.
4. Charles.
5. Mulcahy.
6. Sully.
7. Mulcahy.
8. Radar.
9. Flowers.

EPISODE 7.24 "Ain't Love Grand?"

1. Beethoven.
2. The 8063rd.
3. His class ASU.
4. Bingo.
5. Radar's office.
6. He stands on Hawkeye's cot and beats his chest.
7. "Stormy Weather."

EPISODE 7.25 "The Party"

1. The mess tent.
2. A year.
3. Klinger.
4. Its tires.
5. Kellye.
6. Basketball.

7. Klinger.

SEASON EIGHT

EPISODE 8.1 "Too Many Cooks"

1. He fell into a foxhole.
2. Blue.
3. Spam parmesan.
4. Converse.
5. The stove.
6. Pensacola, FL.

EPISODE 8.2 "Are You Now, Margaret?"

1. An inflated surgical glove.
2. A frog.
3. A Nash.

EPISODE 8.3 "Guerilla My Dreams"

1. Hawkeye.
2. Radar.
3. Klinger.
4. Its own serial number.
5. BJ.

EPISODE 8.4 "Goodbye, Radar: Part 1"

1. Zale.
2. Four bucks.
3. Three.

EPISODE 8.5 "Goodbye, Radar: Part 2"

1. She kisses him.
2. A paddle.
3. "What'd I do wrong now?"
4. Charles.
5. "Never heard of it."
6. Hawkeye's bunk.
7. Potter.

EPISODE 8.6 "Period of Adjustment"

1. Two.
2. Her requisition for more nurses.
3. Soup.
4. Charles.
5. A hippo.
6. He accidently breaks the glass.
7. His helmet.

EPISODE 8.7 "Nurse Doctor"

1. Fifteen.

2. Charles.
3. Francis.

EPISODE 8.8 "Private Finance"

1. A broom.
2. A pitchfork.
3. His chair.
4. Margaret.

EPISODE 8.9 "Mr. and Mrs. Who?"

1. Charles.
2. The Song of Songs.
3. Less than 1%.
4. "Chuck."
5. BJ (or JB Honeydew).
6. A comic book.

EPISODE 8.10 "The Yalu Brick Road"

1. Klinger's turkeys.
2. BJ.
3. Ralph.
4. Fred.
5. BJ.

EPISODE 8.11 "Life Time"

1. Poker.
2. Margaret.
3. Klinger.
4. Margaret.
5. Hawkeye's.
6. Col. Potter.
7. Charles.
8. "Be gentle with me."

EPISODE 8.12 "Dear Uncle Abdul"

1. Hawkeye.
2. A self-portrait of him and Sophie (with Klinger standing in for the colonel).
3. The O Club.
4. Fr. Mulcahy.
5. Hank.
6. Dave.

EPISODE 8.13 "Captains Outrageous"

1. Rosie.
2. Margaret.
3. An abacus.
4. The Pentagon.
5. Hawkeye.

EPISODE 8.14 "Stars and Stripes"

1. Twelve-year-old Scotch.
2. He punched out a superior officer.
3. "Yo-yo."
4. Igor.
5. Klinger.
6. Margaret.

EPISODE 8.15 "Yessir, That's Our Baby"

1. Charles.
2. Hawkeye.
3. Hawkeye and BJ.
4. Klinger.

EPISODE 8.16 "Bottle Fatigue"

1. Bourbon.
2. Cognac.
3. Sparky.
4. "The Leaning Tower of Pompous."

EPISODE 8.17 "Heal Thyself"

1. Hawkeye.
2. The Pusan Perimeter.
3. Gin.
4. "Tolstoy with spurs."

5. Caruso.
6. Potter's.
7. Klinger.

EPISODE 8.18 "Old Soldiers"

1. "The Three Little Pigs."
2. A horse.
3. Fudge.

EPISODE 8.19 "Morale Victory"

1. Popcorn.
2. A suggestion box.
3. A concert pianist.
4. A whip and a chair.
5. Throwing darts.
6. Sand.

EPISODE 8.20 "Lend a Hand"

1. Off-blue.
2. The bubbles.
3. Klinger.
4. Hawkeye.
5. Cheese.

EPISODE 8.21 "Goodbye, Cruel World"

1. He decorates it with things from home.
2. An "Arabian nightmare."
3. Potter's.
4. A pencil.
5. The cheese.
6. Two hours.

EPISODE 8.22 "Dreams"

1. A bridal gown.
2. Peg.
3. A horse.
4. Performs magic tricks for a dying soldier.
5. The pope.
6. Toledo.
7. Kellye.
8. Charles.

EPISODE 8.23 "War Co-Respondent"

1. Twelve-year-old Scotch.
2. A peanut butter sandwich.
3. Baseball.

EPISODE 8.24 "Back Pay"

1. His dad.

2. Rizzo.
3. Moe, Larry, and Curly (The Three Stooges).
4. Margaret.

EPISODE 8.25 "April Fools"

1. A horse.
2. Spring-loaded snakes.
3. Charles.
4. A raccoon's tail.
5. A shot and a beer.
6. Pips.

SEASON NINE

EPISODE 9.1 "The Best of Enemies"

1. Yellow.
2. A boot.
3. Margaret.
4. Klinger.

EPISODE 9.2 "Letters"

1. Irving.
2. Chinchillas.
3. Playing kickball.
4. Soaking his feet.

EPISODE 9.3 "Cementing Relationships"

1. Italy.
2. Charles.
3. Klinger.
4. Charles.

EPISODE 9.4 "Father's Day"

1. Margaret.
2. She salutes him.
3. "Educational Materials."
4. The blood.

EPISODE 9.5 "Death Takes a Holiday"

1. Fudge.
2. An orphanage.
3. "Hawaiian peanuts."

EPISODE 9.6 "A War for All Seasons"

1. Winter.
2. Potter.
3. The Sears catalogue.
4. The gardening section.
5. "Raggmopp."
6. Mulcahy's garden.
7. 8 ½.

8. He creams it.
9. His hat.
10. The Brooklyn Dodgers.
11. A cardboard box.
12. The Giants.

EPISODE 9.7 "Your Retention, Please"

1. Igor.
2. Klinger.
3. The oath of office for the President of the United States.
4. Lady Godiva.

EPISODE 9.8 "Tell It to the Marines"

1. Three days.
2. Holland.
3. "Whistle While You Work."
4. A rose.
5. Pusan.
6. "The Luftwaffe Serenade."

EPISODE 9.9 "Taking the Fifth"

1. The OR.
2. Curare.
3. Five dollars.
4. "Sweet Preserves."
5. The radiator.

EPISODE 9.10 "Operation Friendship"

1. BJ.
2. His nose.
3. His arm.
4. *I, the Jury* by Mickey Spillane.

EPISODE 9.11 "No Sweat"

1. The PA system.
2. TV repair.
3. To get a sleeping pill.
4. Kellye.
5. A slipper.
6. His taxes.
7. Carbon paper.
8. Igor.
9. The showers.

EPISODE 9.12 "Depressing News"

1. *MASH Notes*.
2. Five.
3. Father Mulcahy.

EPISODE 9.13 "No Laughing Matter"

1. *Reader's Digest*.
2. Octopus.

3. Cribbage.

EPISODE 9.14 "Oh, How We Danced"

1. His will.
2. His butterfly collection.
3. Eight months.
4. Hawkeye.
5. Charles.
6. A chair.
7. Margaret.

EPISODE 9.15 "Bottoms Up"

1. Gin.
2. AB-.
3. The Officer's Club.
4. Painting.
5. The nurse's tent.

EPISODE 9.16 "The Red/White Blues"

1. Hawkeye.
2. Tokyo.
3. He thinks Klinger made a mistake when ordering the primaquine.
4. Charles.
5. Mulcahy.

EPISODE 9.17 "Bless You, Hawkeye"

1. A handkerchief.
2. The VIP Tent.
3. Sidney.
4. The O Club.

EPISODE 9.18 "Blood Brothers"

1. Sunday.
2. Mulcahy.
3. Mona.
4. Hawkeye.
5. Father Mulcahy.

EPISODE 9.19 "The Foresight Saga"

1. Hawkeye.
2. "Gentleman farmer."
3. Glasses.
4. Hawkeye.
5. Radar.
6. Potter

EPISODE 9.20 "The Life You Save"

1. The compound.
2. An IV bottle.
3. His hat.

4. BJ.
5. Mulcahy.
6. "I smell bread."

SEASON TEN

EPISODE 10.1 "That's Show Biz"

1. Casualty reports.
2. Father Mulcahy.
3. A guitar.
4. Charles.
5. Pink.
6. Ballet shoes.
7. Charles.
8. Klinger.
9. Groucho Marx.

EPISODE 10.2 "Identity Crisis"

1. Margaret.
2. Hebrew.
3. His cousin, Num-Num.

EPISODE 10.3 "Rumor at the Top"

1. Five.
2. Hawkeye.

3. Hawkeye.
4. Philadelphia.
5. Sha-boom.

EPISODE 10.4 "Give 'Em Hell, Hawkeye"

1. The shape of the conference table.
2. Klinger.
3. BJ.
4. Margaret.

EPISODE 10.5 "Wheelers and Dealers"

1. The mail.
2. Kimpo.
3. Rizzo.
4. A straight.
5. Pink.
6. Igor.
7. Pinball.

EPISODE 10.6 "Communication Breakdown"

1. *Lil' Abner.*
2. Fr. Mulcahy.
3. May 5th.
4. Newspapers.
5. His cot.
6. BJ.
7. Mulcahy's.

8. Potter.

EPISODE 10.7 "Snap Judgement"

1. Penicillin.
2. The Toledo Mud Hens.
3. The carbon paper.
4. Rosie.
5. Charles.

EPISODE 10.8 "Snappier Judgement"

1. Charles.
2. Margaret.
3. Hawkeye and BJ.
4. Hawkeye.
5. "Aspirin, three times a day."

EPISODE 10.9 "'Twas the Day After Christmas"

1. "Jingle Bells."
2. Charles.
3. Potter.
4. Seven.
5. A blizzard.
6. Charles.
7. 48 hours in Seoul.

EPISODE 10.10 "Follies of the Living—Concerns of the Dead"

1. A kidney infection.
2. His grandmother.
3. An IV bottle.
4. A fork.
5. Hicks.
6. Drunk.

EPISODE 10.11 "The Birthday Girls"

1. Margaret.
2. Charles.
3. Charades.
4. Kellye.
5. Klinger.
6. Birthday hats.
7. The Old Missouri Soup Bone.
8. A match.
9. Margaret.

EPISODE 10.12 "Blood and Guts"

1. Kibbee.
2. BJ.
3. An Indian Scout.
4. Hawkeye.
5. Red.

EPISODE 10.13 "A Holy Mess"

1. Margaret.
2. As an omelet.
3. Gillis.
4. In his boots.
5. A picnic.

EPISODE 10.14 "The Tooth Will Set You Free"

1. Combat engineers.
2. Four.
3. Checkers.
4. Ice cream.
5. Charles's.

EPISODE 10.15 "Pressure Points"

1. His shower shoes.
2. White phosphorus rounds.
3. Charles.
4. "Along the Santa Fe Trail."
5. Moe, Larry, and Curly (The Three Stooges).
6. A sock.
7. The creek.
8. Klinger.
9. Records.
10. The Copa.
11. His uncle Roy.

EPISODE 10.16 "Where There's a Will, There's a War"

1. Seoul.
2. Their surgeon was killed.
3. The same spot Hawkeye parked his jeep.
4. His father.
5. His robe.
6. Five cents, and his everlasting respect.
7. His Groucho nose and glasses.
8. His copy of *The Last of the Mohicans*.
9. Hawkeye's Hawaiian shirt.
10. If he finished his will.
11. A list of all the men her father took care of in the war.

EPISODE 10.17 "Promotion Commotion"

1. Being a wino.
2. Col. Potter.
3. Explosive Ordinance Disposal.
4. Sergeant.

EPISODE 10.18 "Heroes"

1. Mulcahy.
2. Twenty.
3. A stroke. "A massive one," according to Hawkeye.
4. "What kind of a guy is Pierce?"
5. Plato and Cavanaugh.

EPISODE 10.19 "Sons and Bowlers"

1. "The Marines' Hymn."
2. Mulcahy lofts the ball.
3. He calls him "Hawkeye."
4. To their fathers and to their sons.

EPISODE 10.20 "Picture This"

1. Hawkeye.
2. "Me and My Shadow."
3. Klinger.

EPISODE 10.21 "That Darn Kid"

1. A vase.
2. $22,340
3. Rizzo.
4. In a brandy snifter.

SEASON ELEVEN

EPISODE 11.1 "Hey, Look Me Over"

1. Packing for a bug out.
2. A can opener.

3. Margaret.
4. Kellye.
5. Kellye.
6. Klinger's office.

EPISODE 11.2 "Trick or Treatment"

1. Charles.
2. A pool ball.
3. Superman.

EPISODE 11.3 "Foreign Affairs"

1. $100,000.
2. Spike Jones.
3. His family wouldn't understand her "bohemian" ways.
4. Don't drink the water.

EPISODE 11.4 "The Joker Is Wild"

1. He nails Hawkeye's boot to the floor.
2. A scamp.
3. A snake.
4. Shaving cream.
5. The 8063rd.
6. The seat of her robe was cut out.
7. Four.
8. A drink.
9. Barbed wire.

EPISODE 11.5 "Who Knew?"

1. Behind the generator shed.
2. Col. Potter.
3. Hawkeye.
4. He reads her diary.

EPISODE 11.6 "Bombshells"

1. Hawkeye.
2. Go fishing.
3. Six.
4. "Hooray for Hollywood."
5. Ted Williams.
6. A heart-shaped box of chocolates.
7. The Bronze Star.

EPISODE 11.7 "Settling Debts"

1. By marriage.
2. A houseboat.
3. Margaret and Mulcahy.
4. White picket.
5. Charles.

EPISODE 11.8 "The Moon Is Not Blue"

1. Potter.
2. A "wino's Erector Set."

3. The beans used to mark the Bingo cards.

EPISODE 11.9 "Run for the Money"

1. A 5 oz. martini.
2. The 8063rd.
3. Loyola.
4. In the camp safe.

EPISODE 11.10 "U.N., the Night, and the Music"

1. France.
2. Hawkeye.
3. Klinger.
4. Backwards.

EPISODE 11.11 "Strange Bedfellows"

1. His son-in-law, Bob.
2. Charles's tape recorder.
3. Tokyo, Japan.
4. His Sunday sermon.
5. Fr. Mulcahy.
6. BJ.

EPISODE 11.12 "Say No More"

1. Seoul.
2. Charles.

3. Harpo.
4. Cutting and squeezing an orange.
5. Hawkeye.
6. A kiss.

EPISODE 11.13 "Friends and Enemies"

1. Margaret.
2. He files down the needle.
3. The O Club.
4. Red.

EPISODE 11.14 "Give and Take"

1. Margaret.
2. Elizabeth Barrett Browning.
3. Darn his socks.
4. Chocolate bars.
5. Ouzo.

EPISODE 11.15 "As Time Goes By"

1. Los Angeles.
2. Igor.
3. A chopper's fan belt.
4. His teddy bear.
5. A fishing lure.

EPISODE 11.16 "Goodbye, Farewell, and Amen"

1. D.
2. Sidney.
3. Blue.
4. Camouflage netting.
5. BJ.
6. Sergeant.
7. Boston Mercy.
8. A motorcycle (with a sidecar).
9. Five.
10. With the POWs.
11. Yellow.
12. Mozart.
13. Fr. Mulcahy.
14. BJ.
15. Cards.
16. Margaret.
17. A mortar barrage.
18. In a row of tires.
19. Hawkeye.
20. Wildfire created by incendiary weapons.
21. A wedding dress (Soon-Lee considers it funeral attire from her culture).
22. Soccer.
23. Mulcahy.
24. A birthday cake.
25. "Falling off a cliff."
26. Potter.
27. "Goodbye."
28. He smashes a record.

29. Performing surgery.
30. Col. Potter.
31. Rizzo.
32. Potter.
33. A book (by Elizabeth Barrett Browning).
34. A garbage truck.
35. They salute him.
36. By helicopter.
37. BJ.
38. GOODBYE.

www.ingramcontent.com/pod-product-compliance
Lightning Source LLC
Chambersburg PA
CBHW051035160426
43193CB00010B/954